A Framework For Understanding Poverty

The mission of **aha!** Process, Inc. is to positively impact the education and lives of individuals in poverty around the world.

Payne, Ruby K., Ph.D.
   A Framework for Understanding Poverty. Second edition, 2005; 78 pp.
   Bibliography p. 78
   ISBN 1-929229-40-2

1. Education   2. Sociology   3. Title

Other selected titles by Ruby K. Payne, Ph.D.

A Framework for Understanding Poverty
Un Marco Para Entender La Pobreza
Understanding Learning
Learning Structures
Preventing School Violence by Creating Emotional Safety: Video Series & Manual
Meeting Standards & Raising Test Scores
      When You Don't Have Much Time or Money: Video Series & Manual (Payne & Magee)
Removing the Mask: Giftedness in Poverty (Slocumb & Payne)
Bridges Out of Poverty: Strategies for Professionals and Communities (Payne, DeVol, & Dreussi Smith)
Think Rather of Zebra (Stailey & Payne)
What Every Church Member Should Know About Poverty (Payne & Ehlig)
Living on a Tightrope: a Survival Handbook for Principals (Payne & Sommers)
Hidden Rules of Class at Work (Payne & Krabill)

Ruby K. Payne, Ph.D.

A Framework for Understanding Poverty

aha! Process, Inc.

Contents

MODULE 1

OVERVIEW AND STATISTICS: KEY POINTS

Workshop Objectives

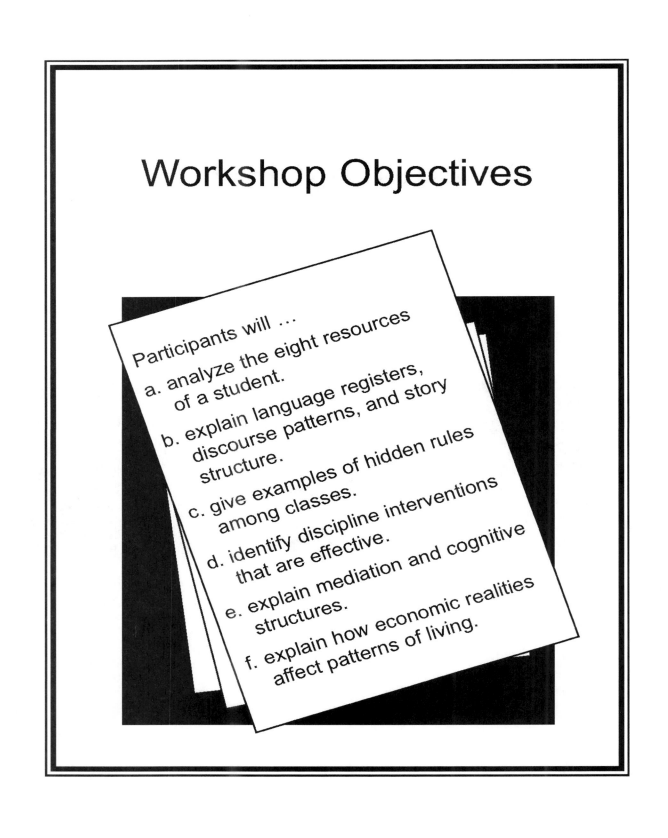

Participants will …

a. analyze the eight resources of a student.

b. explain language registers, discourse patterns, and story structure.

c. give examples of hidden rules among classes.

d. identify discipline interventions that are effective.

e. explain mediation and cognitive structures.

f. explain how economic realities affect patterns of living.

Key Points

1. Poverty is relative.

2. Poverty occurs in all races.

3. Generational and situational poverty are different.

4. This work is based on patterns. All patterns have exceptions.

5. Schools operate from middle class norms and values.

6. Individuals bring with them the hidden rules of the class in which they were raised.

7. There are cultural differences in poverty. This study is cross-cultural and focuses on economics.

8. We must neither excuse them nor scold them. We must teach them.

Key Points

9. We must teach them that there are two sets of rules.

10. To move from poverty to middle class, one must give up (for a period of time) relationships for achievement.

11. Two things that help one move out of poverty are:
    - education
    - relationships

12. Four reasons one leaves poverty are:
    - too painful to stay
    - vision or goal
    - key relationship
    - special talent/skill

www.ahaprocess.com

U.S. MEDIAN INCOME FOR PERSONS AGE 25 AND OLDER BY SEX AND EDUCATIONAL ATTAINMENT: 2003

	Overall	Less Than Ninth Grade	Grades 9 - 12 No Diploma	HS Diploma (includes GED)	Associate Degree	Bachelor's Degree	Master's Degree	Professional Degree	Doctorate
	Numbers of persons with income (in thousands)								
Male	89,558	5,804	7,766	27,889	6,751	16,632	6,157	1,925	1,621
Female	97,319	5,943	8,233	31,921	9,013	17,134	6,451	1,027	801
	Median Income, in 2003 dollars								
Male	$37,288	$18,710	$22,196	$31,411	$40,454	$51,507	$62,495	$100,000	$77,525
Female	$25,499	$12,978	$13,695	$20,759	$26,872	$35,109	$42,466	$56,143	$56,182

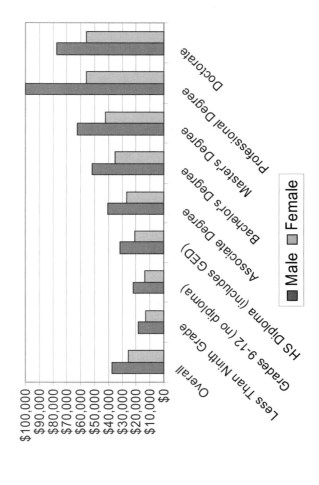

■ Male ▨ Female

Source: U.S. Bureau of the Census

POVERTY STATISTICS

Extreme poverty, poverty, and near poverty rates for children under age 5 by living arrangement, 2003.

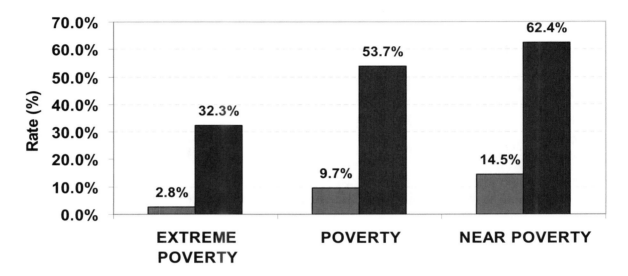

Source: U.S. Bureau of the Census

MODULE 2

RESOURCES

Resources

FINANCIAL
Having the money to purchase goods and services.

EMOTIONAL
Being able to choose and control emotional responses, particularly to negative situations, without engaging in self-destructive behavior. This is an internal resource and shows itself through stamina, perseverance, and choices.

MENTAL
Having the mental abilities and acquired skills (reading, writing, computing) to deal with daily life.

SPIRITUAL
Believing in divine purpose and guidance.

PHYSICAL
Having physical health and mobility.

SUPPORT SYSTEMS
Having friends, family, and backup resources available to access in times of need. These are external resources.

RELATIONSHIPS/ROLE MODELS
Having frequent access to adult(s) who are appropriate, who are **nurturing** to the child, and who do not engage in self-destructive behavior.

KNOWLEDGE OF HIDDEN RULES
Knowing the unspoken cues and habits of a group.

Resource Analysis

Name	Financial resources	Emotional resources	Mental resources	Spiritual resources	Physical resources	Support systems	Relationships/role models	Knowledge of hidden rules

SALLY AND SUEANN

BACKGROUND

Sally is an 8-year-old white girl whose mother, SueAnn, has been married and divorced twice. Her mother works two jobs and does not receive child support. An older sister is pregnant. Sally has two stepsiblings—one younger and one older. The current stepfather's favorite child is the youngest, a son. The stepfather is laid off right now.

You are Sally's mother, SueAnn, a 33-year-old white female. You are on your third marriage. You have four children by four different men. You are working two jobs right now because your current husband has been laid off. He is supposed to be taking care of the kids, but he doesn't like to be tied down. You got pregnant when you were a senior in high school, so you were unable to finish school. You knew who the father was, but he changed his mind and wouldn't marry you. You kept the child, and she is now 15 and pregnant. Your second child is Sally and she is 8 years old. Between the two jobs you bring home about $400 a week, and you are exhausted. You make the girls cook and clean. You are very tired. Lately you and your husband have been fighting a lot. Your mother and father are divorced and live in the same town that you do. You remember how much you loved to dance country-western and party. All you wish for now is sleep. You may have to move again soon because you're so far behind on the bills.

CURRENT SITUATION

You get a call at work. You let your husband drop you off at work because he was going to fix the muffler. Your husband is now in jail. He was caught driving while intoxicated. This is the second time he has been caught. You need $500 to pay the bondsman to get him out of jail. Furthermore, he was driving your car, which didn't have insurance. They have towed the car and the towing bill is $80. Each day it's impounded it will cost you $40 in parking fees, and you can't get the car out until you have proof of insurance. When and if your husband gets out of jail, he will need to see the probation officer, which will cost him $60 each visit.

Your pregnant daughter needs $400 to pay the doctor so that he will keep seeing her. You have told her she needs to go to the clinic where the service is free. However, the wait is usually three to four hours, and she misses a half day of school. There is also the problem of getting her there. It's in a bad part of town, and it will be dark before you can get there to pick her up.

The bill collector calls you at work and tells you he is going to take you to court for overdue electric bills at the last place you lived. You now live in an apartment where the utilities are paid, but you are behind on your rent by a month. You were okay until your husband got laid off. You are out of birth-control pills. To refill the prescription, you have to go to the clinic and wait three to four hours, and you can't take that much time off work. Also, you need $20 for the birth-control pills. Lately your husband has been looking at Sally in ways that you don't like. But you are so tired.

What are Sally and SueAnn's resources? Below, put a check under the resources that are present, a minus under the ones that are not, and a question mark where the resources are uncertain.

Name	Financial resources	Emotional resources	Mental resources	Spiritual resources	Physical resources	Support systems	Relationships/role models	Knowledge of hidden rules

OTIS AND VANGIE

BACKGROUND

Otis is a 9-year-old black boy. His mother conceived him at 14, dropped out of school, and is on welfare. Otis has two younger siblings and one older sibling who is a gang member.

You are Otis's mother, Vangie. You are a 24-year-old black female. You were the oldest of five children. You had your first child when you were 13. You have received welfare and food stamps since the birth of your first child. You lived with your mother until your fourth child was born when you were 18. Then you got your own place. You dropped out of school when you were pregnant with Otis. School was always difficult for you, and you never did feel comfortable reading much anyway. Your current boyfriend comes often and he works sometimes. Your mother lives down the street. Your weekly income (including food stamps) is $215. You move a lot because there are always more bills at the end of the month than money.

CURRENT SITUATION

Your sister calls and tells you that her boyfriend has beaten her again, and she needs to come spend the night at your house. The last time she came she stayed for two weeks, and her 12-year-old handicapped son would not leave your 5-year-old daughter alone. You have several choices: (1) You could take her in and make her pay for her meals, (2) you could not take her in and have the whole family mad at you, (3) you could tell your daughter to hit her cousin when he comes close, (4) you could make Otis take care of the handicapped son, (5) you could slap the fool out of the handicapped son, (6) you could use the rent money to pay for the extra food, (7) you could go partying together and let Otis take care of the kids, or (8) you could move to a bigger place.

Otis comes home from school and announces that the school is going to have a reading contest. For every five books you read to him, he will receive a coupon to get $2 off a pizza. To obtain his books, he needs you to go to the library. Also, you aren't sure you can even read to him because your skills were never good, and you haven't read for a long time. Getting to the library requires that you walk because you don't have a car. There were two drive-by shootings last week. He also tells you that the school is having an open house and is sending a bus around the neighborhood to pick up parents. He gives you a note that you can't read.

You are probably going to have to move again. This week Otis got cut badly at school, and the school nurse took him to the emergency room; they want $200. Rent is due for the month, and it's $300 for three bedrooms. Sister is coming, and that means extra food because she never has any money. Your boyfriend got arrested and wants you to get him out of jail. He was arrested for assault. The bondsman wants $500. Your ex-boyfriend knew better than to come around. You need your boyfriend because his money makes it possible to keep from going hungry.

The teacher calls and tells you that Otis is misbehaving again. You beat the fool out of him with a belt and tell him he better behave. But that night you fix him his favorite dinner, then you tell everyone you talk to how Otis is misbehaving and what a burden he is to you.

What are Otis and Vangie's resources? Below put a check under the resources that are present, a minus under the ones that are not, and a question mark where the resources are uncertain.

Name	Financial resources	Emotional resources	Mental resources	Spiritual resources	Physical resources	Support systems	Relationships/role models	Knowledge of hidden rules

JOHN AND ADELE

BACKGROUND

John is an 8-year-old white boy. His father is a doctor and remarried but does not see his children. He pays minimal child support. The mother, Adele, works part-time and is an alcoholic. One younger sibling, a girl who is mentally and physically handicapped, lives with the mother and John.

You are Adele, John's mother. You are a 29-year-old white female. You quit college your sophomore year so that you could go to work to support John's father as he went through medical school. You were both elated when John was born. During the time your husband was an intern, you found that a drink or two or three in the evening calmed you down, especially since your husband was gone so much. When your second child was born, she was severely handicapped. Both of you were in shock. A year later your husband finished his residency, announced that he was in love with another woman, and divorced you. Last you heard, your husband is driving a Porsche, and he and his new wife spent their most recent vacation in Cancun. Your parents are dead. You have a sister who lives 50 miles away. Your weekly income, including child support, is $300 before taxes. Your handicapped child is 3 years old and is in day care provided by the school district.

CURRENT SITUATION

You have been late to work for the third time this month. Your car broke down, and it will take $400 to fix it. Your boss told you that you will be docked for a day's pay—and that if you're late again, you will be fired. You don't know how you're going to get to work tomorrow. You consider several choices: (1) You can go car shopping, (2) you can put the car in the garage and worry about the money later, (3) you can invite the mechanic over for dinner, (4) you can get mad and quit, (5) you can call your ex and threaten to take him back to court unless he pays for the car, (6) you can get a second job, or (7) you can get drunk.

Your daughter has had another seizure, and you took her to the doctor (one of the reasons you were late for work). The new medicine will cost you $45 every month.

John comes home from school and announces that the school is going to have a reading contest. Every book you read with him will earn points for him. Each book is one point, and he wants to earn 100 points. You must do physical therapy with your daughter each evening for 30 minutes, as well as get dinner. For John to get his books, he needs you to go to the library with him. You have only enough gas to go to work and back for the rest of the week, maybe not that. He also tells you that the school is having an open house, and he will get a pencil if you come. But John is not old enough to watch your daughter. Your ex has already threatened to bring up in court that you are an unfit mother if you try to get more money from him.

The mechanic calls and invites you out to dinner. He tells you that you might be able to work something out in terms of payment. It has been a long time since you have been out, and he is good-looking and seems like a nice man.

What are Adele and John's resources? Below put a check under the resources that are present, a minus under the ones that are not, and a question mark where the resources are uncertain.

Name	Financial resources	Emotional resources	Mental resources	Spiritual resources	Physical resources	Support systems	Relationships/role models	Knowledge of hidden rules

OPIE AND OPRAH

BACKGROUND

Opie is a 12-year-old African-American girl and the oldest of five children. She runs the household because her mother, Oprah, works long hours as a domestic. Grandmother, who is 80, is senile and lives with them, as well as an out-of-work uncle.

You are Opie's mother, Oprah. You are a 32-year-old African-American female. You were married for 10 years to your husband, and then he was killed in a car accident on the way to work two years ago. You work long hours as a domestic for a doctor. You go to the Missionary Baptist Church every Sunday where you lead the choir. Your employer treats you well and you take home about $300 every week. You ride public transportation to work and the church bus on Sunday. You want your children to go to college, even though you only finished high school.

CURRENT SITUATION

Your employer gives you a $400 Christmas bonus. You thank the Lord at church for the gift. After church, three different people approach you privately. One asks for $50 to have the electricity turned on; one asks for $100 to feed her brother's family; one asks for $60 to replace a pair of broken glasses. You were hoping to save some money for an emergency.

Opie has the opportunity to be in a state-sponsored competition that requires after-school practices. You want her to do that, but you must have her at home after school every day.

What resources do Opie and Oprah have? On p. 9 put a check under the resources that are present, a minus under the ones that are not, and a question mark where the resources are uncertain.

WISTERIA AND EILEEN

BACKGROUND

Eileen is a 10-year-old white girl who lives with her 70-year-old grandmother, Wisteria, who is on Social Security. Eileen doesn't know who her father is. Her mother has been arrested four times for prostitution and/or drug possession in the last two years. About once a year Mother sobers up for a month and wants Eileen back as her child.

You are Eileen's grandmother, Wisteria. You get about $150 a week from Social Security. Your daughter, Eileen's mother, has been in trouble for years. You have given up on her, and you couldn't stand to see Eileen in a foster home, so you have taken her into your home. Eileen's mother was never sure who the father was; she is a drug addict and has been arrested frequently. One of her various pimps or boyfriends usually gets her out of jail. Once a year, when she sobers up for a short period of time, she gives Eileen lots of attention and then leaves. The last time she came and left, Eileen cried and cried and said she never wanted to see her mother again. You have a little money in savings but you don't want to use it yet. Your house is paid for and you have a decent car. You worry about what will happen to Eileen if you get sick or die, and you pray each day to live until Eileen is 18. You don't see as well as you once did. All your relatives are either dead or distant. Every Sunday you and Eileen go to the United Methodist Church where you have been a member for 40 years.

CURRENT SITUATION

Eileen comes home from school with an assigned project. She must do a family history and interview as many relatives as possible. You aren't sure what to say to Eileen.

The teacher tells you at a conference that Eileen has an imaginary friend whom she talks to a great deal during the day. The teacher recommends that you seek counseling for Eileen. She knows a counselor who would charge only $40 a session. She also comments that Eileen's clothes are old-fashioned and that she doesn't fit in very well with the other students. You don't tell the teacher that you make Eileen's clothes. The teacher suggests that you let Eileen have friends over so she can socialize, but you don't know if anyone would come—or if you could stand the noise.

What are Eileen and Wisteria's resources? On p. 9 put a check under the resources that are present, a minus under the ones that are not, and a question mark where the resources are uncertain.

JUAN AND RAMON

BACKGROUND

Juan is a 6-year-old Hispanic boy who lives with his uncle Ramón. Juan's father was killed in a gang-related shooting. His uncle is angry about the death of Juan's father. When his uncle is not around, Juan stays with his grandmother, who speaks no English. The uncle makes his living selling drugs but is very respectful toward his mother.

You are Juan's uncle, Ramón, a 25-year-old Hispanic male. You doubt that you will live many more years because you know that most of the people like you are either dead or in jail. You are angry. Your brother, Juan's father, was killed by a rival gang two years ago when Juan was 4. Juan is your godchild, and you will defend him with your blood. Juan's mother was a piece of white trash and wouldn't take care of Juan like a good mother should. She is in jail now for gang-related activities. You leave Juan with your mother often because the activities you're involved in are too dangerous to have Juan along. You are a leader in your gang and sell drugs as well. Your mother speaks only Spanish, but you have taught Juan to be very respectful toward her. She goes to mass every Sunday and takes Juan with her when she can. You make $1,000 a week on average.

CURRENT SITUATION

Juan comes home with a notice about a parent-teacher conference. You are away, hiding from the police. Grandmother cannot read Spanish or English.

The rival gang has killed another one of your gang members. This has forced you to be away from Juan more that you would like. Plans are that you will kill the leader of the rival gang, but then you will need to go to Mexico for some time to hide. You are thinking about taking Juan with you because he is all in the world that you love. You are stockpiling money. You don't want to take him out of school, but he is only 6; he can catch up. You don't think you'll live past 30, and you want to have time with him.

What resources do Juan and Ramón have? On p. 9 put a check under the resources that are present, a minus under the ones that are not, and a question mark where the resources are uncertain.

MARIA AND NOEMI

BACKGROUND

Maria is a 10-year-old Hispanic girl. Her mother does not drive or speak English. Father speaks some English. Maria is a second-generation Hispanic born in the United States. Mother does not work outside the home. Father works for minimum wage as a concrete worker. There are five children. The family gets food stamps, and the mother is a devout Catholic.

You are Maria's mother, Noemi. You are a 27-year-old Hispanic female. You have five children. You have been married to your husband for 11 years and you love him and your children very much. Children always come first. As a child, you and your parents were migrant workers, so you are happy that you have a place to live and do not need to move around. Because of the migrant work, you didn't go past the sixth grade. Your husband works on a construction crew laying concrete. When it's not raining and when there's plenty of building, he has lots of work. Sometimes, though, he will go two or three weeks with no work and, therefore, no money. Your parents live in your town, and they try to help you when times are bad. You get food stamps to help out. You go to mass every Sunday, and often on weekends you go to your parents' place with your children and brothers and sisters. Your husband is a good man, and he loves his children. On a good week he will bring home $400.

CURRENT SITUATION

Maria comes home and says she has to do a salt map. You have just spent all the money for the week on food—and she needs five pounds of flour, two pounds of salt, and a piece of board to put it on. She also needs to get information from an encyclopedia, whatever that is. The car has broken down and will require $100 for parts. The baby is sick, and medicine will be $30. It has rained for two weeks, and your husband hasn't had any work or pay.

The teacher has asked Maria to stay after school and be in an academic contest. You expect her to get married and have children just as you have. But for now you need her to help you with the children.

What resources do Maria and Noemi have? On p. 9 put a check under the resources that are present, a minus under the ones that are not, and a question mark where the resources are uncertain.

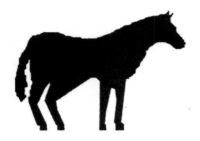

TIJUANA CHECOSOVAKIA

BACKGROUND

You are a 14-year-old African-American female. Your mother named you Tijuana Checosovakia because she heard that on television and liked the name. You had your first child at 11 years of age and your second one at 13 years of age. You are now a freshman in high school.

You live in a rural area and go to the local high school. There are several state schools for juvenile delinquents in the area, and you like to hang around the fences and look at the boys.

CURRENT SITUATION

Last month your mother found out that she was pregnant. Your 15-year-old sister is pregnant also. You sure are glad you aren't pregnant right now because they are so moody.

You are in a family literacy program as a part of the requirement for receiving state aid. Last week you and the other teenage mothers in this program were to go to an amusement park with the babies as a way of learning to engage in family activities. But neither you nor the other girls are fools. You left your babies at home and wore your tightest clothes. Those teachers made you go back home, change clothes, and bring the babies. So stupid!

Last week was the first day you were back in school again. You come to school because it is a part of this family literacy requirement. The principal made you take out your nose ring. You demanded that she find you a broomstraw so that you could put it in your nose to keep that hole open. You paid good money for that nose piercing. And then that principal is so dumb. She told you that you would look funny with the broomstick sticking out of your nose. She didn't even know that you just burn the end off and it keeps the hole open. You wonder how that principal stays alive.

And then the counselor wants to know why you got pregnant and why the fathers were listed as unknown. You told the counselor that you didn't want the babies' fathers involved. Those are your babies—only yours.

What are Tijuana Checosovakia's resources? On p. 9 put a check under the resources that are present, a minus under the ones that are not, and a question mark where the resources are uncertain.

HABIB

BACKGROUND

You are an African-American male, age 18. The reason you come to school is that it is a condition of your probation. You are not really a bad person. It just seems that you are always at the wrong place at the wrong time. You don't have a malicious bone in your body; you are likable and easily persuaded. Your one great attribute is that you are one heck of a fighter. The girls like you. You played on the football team, but you just couldn't keep up the grades. And besides, girls were much more fun than football.

You went on probation when you were 16. You and the boys were looking for something to do, so you broke into the local pawnshop. It was one of those days that just was no good. You had come home from school and found your mama beaten up by her latest boyfriend. Shirley, your younger sister, had taken her two babies and left. You called an ambulance for your mother, but you didn't go to the hospital. She will miss a couple days of work because of the beating. You would like to help with the money, but you can't get a job because of your arrest and the fact that you are on probation for armed robbery.

So you were mad when you went looking for the boyfriend. Your girlfriend was mad at you; so breaking into the pawnshop sounded like a good idea at the time. But you got caught and were charged with armed robbery. Juan had loaned you his gun and you had put it into your pocket.

CURRENT SITUATION

You are in alternative school. You can read fairly well. You like people and enjoy being with them. But in your heart you are scared for your younger brother. As you wrote to the teacher one day, "I want my little brother to be successful in life. I want him to be the best he can be in whatever he wants to do. But I know I don't want him to hang in the streets, 'cause the streets are not going to lead a good life for him. I know from experience 'cause I rapped up in the streets, and it ain't cool. All the cool ones dead. It's all based on money. Money run the system, so I'm gonna make sure I have plenny of that."

What are Habib's resources? On p. 9 put a check under the resources that are present, a minus under the ones that are not, and a question mark where the resources are uncertain.

GERALDO

BACKGROUND

You are a Hispanic male, 13 years old, and you are in seventh grade. You are a prominent gang member. It's a matter of pride. When you were 11 you watched your 18-year-old cousin put a gun in his mouth and shoot himself. Your other cousin, who was 17 at the time, ran out of the room and killed himself by running his car under an 18-wheeler.

Your mother attends mass every Saturday, and you love her. You know the rules of the house; however, the street is different. Last week your gang made $4,000 selling drugs. This money was split among 10 members.

CURRENT SITUATION

Today is the anniversary of your cousins' deaths. You took a little acid before you went to school today. It seemed like the only way to face school. You really like your reading teacher, but all you could do was giggle. It sure beats crying. You haven't turned in your assignments for the last two weeks, but then again, you could do almost all the assignments with one hand tied behind your back if you felt like it.

You are watching your back. Today a police officer was at school doing an assembly on drugs. He watched you, and you watched him. Rumor has it that there will be a fight between your gang and another rival gang soon.

But today in particular you watched Tony at lunch. Tony's dad drives a Mercedes and drops him off every morning at school. You wonder what it must be like to have money and not worry about dying. There is no reason to do well in school; you know you are going to be dead before you're 25. You might as well enjoy life and girls. As you wrote to your teacher, "I would like adults to know that people my age are different than when they came up. They grew up different than I did. I grew up with sex, money, and murder and banging in the streets and that's not all. They expect me to do what they want. Well, what they want at home is easy, but as soon as I leave those four walls of home sweet home comes the hard life. As soon as I'm in the streets, it turns into a nightmare, not like my house. It makes me want to die and to get away from the violence. I guess that's why I have no one, because faithful is not in my vocabulary. I'm only faithful to them streets."

What are Geraldo's resources? On p. 9 put a check under the resources that are present, a minus under the ones that are not, and a question mark where the resources are uncertain.

STEVE

BACKGROUND

You are a 17-year-old white male, a senior in high school. For as long as you can remember, your father has been a mean drunk. But you haven't been home since you were 14, when he kicked you out. Your mother cried and cried, but then he beat her into silence.

You remember the night you were kicked out. You had no place to go, so you slept on the church steps because you believed you would be safe there. You rummaged food from the garbage bins of the fast-food restaurants. You kept on going to school because at least you were safe there. You got a job at a restaurant, even though you were underage, and you got a cheap apartment after a couple of months.

CURRENT SITUATION

At 16 you got a full-time job working in the evenings for minimum wage. There's a counselor at school who keeps track of you and how you're doing in school. This week he came with a stack of homework that you need to do in math. Your brother is living with you now as well. You have told the counselor that you think you will just quit. You are so discouraged, and the math teacher told you in front of the class yesterday that anyone who was a senior and still in Algebra I might as well drop out of school.

But the counselor told you he was counting on you. He knew it was rough, but he knew you could do it. So you agreed to do the homework for the counselor. God knows you hate the algebra teacher. The counselor told you to come by at 7 o'clock in the morning, and he would help you with the algebra.

There are no girls in your life. All you have time to do is go to work, go to school, and sleep.

What are Steve's resources? On p. 9 put a check under the resources that are present, a minus under the ones that are not, and a question mark where the resources are uncertain.

MAGNOLIA

BACKGROUND

You are in the 10th grade and are a white female, 16 years old. You barely made it to school on time today because you had to get your eight brothers and sisters ready for school. Your mother didn't come home last night and you aren't sure where she is. You just hope and pray you get to the mailbox before she does when the welfare check comes in. Two weeks ago you called in sick so that you could wait and get the mail. Then you lied to your mother and said the check hadn't come. But there was no food in the house, and you couldn't let your brothers and sisters starve.

Your grades are B's and C's and you feel happy about that. You could get straight A's if you had time to do your projects. You ace most of the tests, but you don't have time to do the homework. One of the teachers last week told you that you were bright but lazy. You didn't say anything. How could you begin to explain? The only things that are constant in your life are your brothers and sisters, who have five different fathers.

You can't remember a time that you didn't take care of them. You remember when you used to steal from the people you baby sat for because your mother told you to do that. But it just made you feel dirty, so you refused to steal, even when that meant you had to go hungry. You can't remember a time when you haven't been hungry sometime during a week.

You want to be a teacher. You remember your fifth-grade teacher who brought you a turkey and meal on Thanksgiving. You were so grateful because there had been no food. You believe that if you were a teacher you could help kids also.

CURRENT SITUATION

The teacher is lecturing on the civilization of Greece and you are interested, but you are wondering what is happening at home. You left your 4-year-old brother alone because you couldn't miss any more school this six weeks, and your mother still wasn't home. But he has stayed at home alone before.

Last night Sally cried because she didn't have three dollars to go on the field trip. Johnny cried because he couldn't go to a birthday party. You don't have a car. The girls in P.E. today laughed at you because you are fat, but you know that fat might keep you alive. You have to eat when it's there. Besides, you have no desire to be attractive to boys. You know what it can do. The girls right now are passing notes about their dates. You just want to make sure your 4-year-old brother is OK.

What are Magnolia's resources? On p. 9 put a check under the resources that are present, a minus under the ones that are not, and a question mark where the resources are uncertain.

www.ahaprocess.com

TAHITI AND THERESA

BACKGROUND

You are Tahiti, age 14. Your father was an African-American, and your mother was from Mexico. Theresa is your best friend. She is also 14. Her mother was from Mexico, and her father was from Puerto Rico. You each want to have a baby. School has never been easy for you or for Theresa, so all you talk about are boys.

Theresa has been luckier than you have been. Both of you have been trying since you were 13 to get pregnant. Both of you are very pretty, and you each have a boyfriend. But Theresa is luckier than you. She and her boyfriend, Miguel, have been having sex at least twice a week for a month now. Miguel is a member of the toughest gang on the streets, and he is a real homeboy. But your boyfriend, Raul, only wants to make love after he has been drinking, and then he's rough.

Lately one of the rival gang members, Gilberto, is looking at you and has touched you in the hall when Raul wasn't looking. But you know Raul and the gang would hurt him. You want a baby so much.

CURRENT SITUATION

Today in class the teacher moved Gilberto so that he now sits next to you. He wrote you a note asking to meet you after school at a certain place. You tell him yes because you want to make love. You want a baby, and you want Raul to know that he can't be messing around all the time with your love. Besides, it has been boring lately.

Your father works at the refinery and brings home about $600 a week. Your mother stays at home. But last night they had a knock-down fight; he had been drinking. You left the house for a while.

You are failing in school. School really doesn't matter because you're going to have a baby and stay at home just like your mother did. There is no other way. Meanwhile, you hope you can get pregnant before Theresa does. Then you will have something of your own.

What are Tahiti's resources? On p. 9 put a check under the resources that are present, a minus under the ones that are not, and a question mark where the resources are uncertain.

RAQUEL

BACKGROUND

You are Raquel, a 15-year-old white female. You are about 5-feet-6 and 140 pounds. You are intelligent and cynical and could pass as a 20-year-old. You have been on your own for a long time. Right now you are in alternative school. You just can't handle regular high school.

When you were 11 your father and mother divorced. Your parents made more than $100,000 a year before the divorce, but even then they both did drugs—cocaine, designer drugs, etc. Then when you were 11 the divorce happened, and you and your sister, who was 4 at the time, went with your father as a part of the custody settlement. He moved with you to a city several hundred miles away. His drug habit caught up with him, and he drank alcohol daily. In fact, he was drunk most of the time. His only job was selling cocaine and marijuana, and he couldn't even keep up with that. You knew that if you didn't do something, you and your sister would starve. You went to school every day so that you weren't taken away from your father—you didn't want to go back to your mother—but at night you made the sales that he couldn't make during the day. At age 12 you bought a car on your own and drove so that you could make the deliveries. You made sure your sister was taken care of and got to kindergarten. You didn't tell anyone. But some days you didn't learn much at school because you were so tired. It was a good thing school wasn't hard for you.

Your father was arrested when you were 14, and you went to live with relatives. You returned to regular high school, but one day one of the students made a comment about your father being in jail. You were so angry you couldn't see straight. But then you heard one of the high school boys talking about your 8-year-old sister and how she would be a good lay, and you beat the _____ out of him. You knew how many men you had to fight off yourself during the drug days. That's how you got into alternative school. All you really love is your sister, and you intend to make sure she doesn't live through your hell.

CURRENT SITUATION

You live with your grandmother (your father's mother). She didn't particularly want you, but your father made her promise. There is not much money, and you can't legally drive yet, even though you know how. Yesterday, when you got home, Grandmother was watching the soap operas and the house was a pigsty. A clean house is really important to you, and you kept yours clean when you were in charge. You can't say anything because Grandmother gets angry. So you cleaned it up. Someone was in your room also, going through your things. But you can't say anything. One of her sons is living there right now because his wife kicked him out; you keep an eagle eye on your sister.

Today at school one of the teachers took 40 points away from you because you told Todd, the dumb 19-year-old who sits next to you, to _____ off because he wanted to know if you would be "available" for $20. It seems like the teacher doesn't even have a clue about what the homeboys mean when they're talking or what goes on in her class. Sylvia, the 18-year-old in your class who is a stripper, thinks she might be pregnant and asks you what to do. You look in her eyes and see your own reflection and wonder how you ever got mixed up with this group. You are so lonely and wonder if this is all life has to offer and what you ever did to deserve this. You remember better times but know you'll have to go to college to get out of this situation. But you wonder how long you can stand all the stupid people around you. You can't commit suicide because you love your younger sister and must be there for her. You're counting the days until you're 18, because then you'll be free.

What are Raquel's resources? On p. 9 put a check under the resources that are present, a minus under the ones that are not, and a question mark where the resources are uncertain.

MODULE 3

LANGUAGE, STORY STRUCTURE, COGNITION

Registers of Language

REGISTER	EXPLANATION
FROZEN	Language that is always the same. For example: Lord's Prayer, wedding vows, etc.
FORMAL	The standard sentence syntax and word choice of work and school. Has complete sentences and specific word choice.
CONSULTATIVE	Formal register when used in conversation. Discourse pattern not quite as direct as formal register.
CASUAL	Language between friends characterized by a 400- to 800-word vocabulary. Word choice general and not specific. Conversation dependent upon non-verbal assists. Sentence syntax often incomplete.
INTIMATE	Language between lovers or twins. Language of sexual harassment.

Cognitive Strategies

INPUT:
Quantity gathered and
quality of data gathered

1. Use planning behaviors.
2. Focus perception on a specific stimulus.
3. Control impulsivity.
4. Explore data systematically.
5. Use appropriate and accurate labels.
6. Organize space using stable systems of reference.
7. Orient data in time.
8. Identify constancies across variations.
9. Gather precise and accurate data.
10. Consider two sources of information at once.
11. Organize data (parts of a whole).
12. Visually transport data.

1. Identify and define the problem.
2. Select relevant cues.
3. Compare data.
4. Select appropriate categories of time.
5. Summarize data.
6. Project relationship of data.
7. Use logical data.
8. Test hypothesis.
9. Build inferences.
10. Make a plan using the data.
11. Use appropriate labels.
12. Use data systematically.

ELABORATION:
Efficient use of data

OUTPUT:
Communication of
elaboration and input

1. Communicate clearly the labels and processes.
2. Visually transport data correctly.
3. Use precise and accurate language.
4. Control impulsive behavior.

Adapted from work of Reuven Feuerstein

IF AN INDIVIDUAL DEPENDS UPON A RANDOM, EPISODIC STORY STRUCTURE FOR MEMORY PATTERNS, LIVES IN AN UNPREDICTABLE ENVIRONMENT, AND HAS NOT DEVELOPED THE ABILITY TO PLAN, THEN …

IF AN INDIVIDUAL CANNOT PLAN, HE OR SHE CANNOT PREDICT.

IF AN INDIVIDUAL CANNOT PREDICT, HE OR SHE CANNOT IDENTIFY CAUSE AND EFFECT.

IF AN INDIVIDUAL CANNOT IDENTIFY CAUSE AND EFFECT, HE OR SHE CANNOT IDENTIFY CONSEQUENCE.

IF AN INDIVIDUAL CANNOT IDENTIFY CONSEQUENCE, HE OR SHE CANNOT CONTROL IMPULSIVITY.

IF AN INDIVIDUAL CANNOT CONTROL IMPULSIVITY, HE OR SHE _____.

MEDIATION

Identification of the stimulus	Assignment of meaning	Identification of a strategy

MODULE 4

FAMILY STRUCTURE

CASE STUDY (Bold type indicates the narrator; plain type indicates comments from various participants. Names have been changed to protect the girl.)

WALTER (white male)

As the story would be told in poverty ... probably by a relative or neighbor:

Well, you know Walter got put away for 37 years. Him being 48 and all. He'll probably die in jail. Just couldn't leave his hands off that 12-year-old Susie. Dirty old man. Bodding's gonna whup his tail. **Already did. You know Bodding was waiting for him in jail and beat the living daylights out of him already.** In jail? **Yeah, Bodding got caught for possession. Had $12,000 on him when they caught him.** Golly, wish I was there to cash in! (laughter) A man's gotta make a living! **Susie being blind and all, I can see why Bodding beat the daylights out of Walter. Lucky he didn't get killed, old Walter is.** Too bad her momma is no good. **She started the whole thing! Susie's momma goes over there and argues with Bodding.** Ain't they divorced? **Yeah, and she's got Walter working for her, repairing her house or something!** Or something, I bet. What she got in her house that's worth repairing? **Anyway, she goes over to Bodding's house to take the lawnmower,** I reckon so as Walter can mow the yard? I bet that's the first time old Walter has ever broken a sweat! Reminds me of the time I saw Walter thinking about taking a job. All that thinking, and he had to get drunk. He went to jail that time too—a felony, I think it was—so many of those DWIs. Judge told him he was egregious. Walter said he wasn't greasy—he took a bath last week! (laughter) **Bodding and momma got in a fight, so she tells Walter to take Susie with him.** Lordy—her elevator must not go all the way to the top! Didn't she know about him gettin' arrested for enticing a minor? **And Susie blind and all. And she sends Susie with Walter?** She sure don't care about her babies. **Well, Walter's momma was there 'cause Walter lives with his momma seein' as how he can't keep no job.** Ain't his other brother there? **Yeah, and him 41 years old. That poor woman sure has her burdens to bear. And then her 30-year-old daughter, Susie's momma, at home too. You know Susie's momma lost custody of her kids. Walter gets these videos, you know. Those adult videos. Heavy breathing!** (laughter) Some of those are more fun to listen to than look at! (laughter) Those people in the videos are des-per-ate! **Anyway, he puts**

those on and then carries Susie in his room and tells her she wants him—and describes all his sex-u-al exploits! Golly, he must be a loooooooooover—all he does is talk about it. (laughter) He should be shot. I'd kill him if he did that to my kid! **Then he lets his fingers do the walking.** Kinda like the yellow pages! (laughter) **I guess he didn't do anything with his 'thang,' according to Miss Rosie who went to that trial every day. And Susie begging him to stop so many times.** Probably couldn't do anything with it—that's why he needs to listen to the breathing! Pant! Pant! (laughter) What a no-'count, low-down creep. I'll pay Bodding to kill him! **I hear tell that, according to Bodding, the only way Walter is coming out of jail is in a pine box.** Don't blame him, myself. **Yeah, Miss Rosie said Walter's momma said at the trial that the door to Walter's room was open, and there ain't no way Walter could have done that. That she is a good Christian momma, and she don't put up with that.** Oh Lordy, did God strike her dead on the spot or is she still alive? I'd be afraid of being in eternal hell for telling a story like that! **Miss Rosie said that her 12-year-old nephew who was there at the trial testified that the door was closed, and his grandma told him to say it was open!** Ooo! Oo! Oo! That poor baby tells the truth? His grandma gonna make him mis-er-a-ble! **And then Walter's momma tells that jury that she never allows those adult videos in her house, leastways not that she pays for it!** (lots of laughter) I bet the judge bit on that one! How is Walter gonna get videos except for her money? Mowing yards? (more laughter) No, I bet he saves his pennies! (laughter) **All these years she has covered for Walter. Guess she just couldn't cover no more.** Remember that time Walter got drunk and wrecked her car, and she said she was driving? And she was at the hospital with a broken leg and when the judge asked her how she could be driving and in the hospital simultaneously? And she said that's just how it was—simultaneously—she had never felt so excited in her life? (laughter) Who turned Walter in? **Well it wasn't Susie's momma. She's busy with Skeeter, her new boyfriend. I hear he's something.** Remember that one boyfriend she had? Thought he was smart? **Speaking of smart—that Susie sure is. Her blind and all, and she won the district spelling bee for the seventh grade this year. I hear she's in National Honor Society, whatever that is.** Wonder if it's kinda like the country club. Instead of playing golf, you just spell! (laughter) **Susie calls this friend of hers who tells her mother, and they come and get her and take her to the police and hospital.** Some rich lady not minding her own business, that's for sure. **Well, it was a good thing for Susie, 'cause that Momma of hers sure ain't good for Susie. She don't deserve a kid like Susie. SHE oughta be blind.** Ain't that the truth. Way I see it, she already is—look at Skeeter! (lots of laughter)

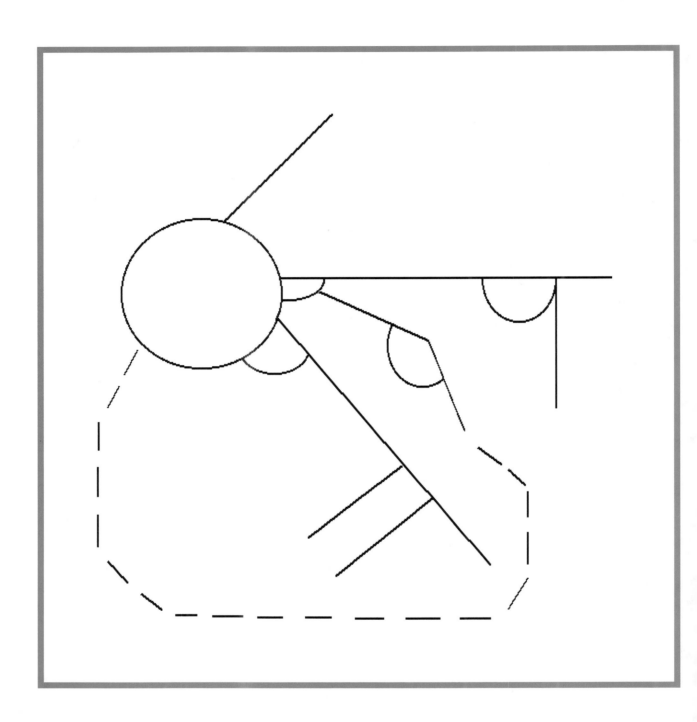

www.ahaprocess.com

MODULE 5

HIDDEN RULES

Could you survive in poverty?

COMPLETE THE QUIZ:
Put a check by each item you know how to do.

_____ 1.   I know which churches and sections of town have the best rummage sales.

_____ 2.   I know which rummage sales have "bag sales" and when.

_____ 3.   I know which grocery stores' garbage bins can be accessed for thrown-away food.

_____ 4.   I know how to get someone out of jail.

_____ 5.   I know how to physically fight and defend myself physically.

_____ 6.   I know how to get a gun, even if I have a police record.

_____ 7.   I know how to keep my clothes from being stolen at the Laundromat.

_____ 8.   I know what problems to look for in a used car.

_____ 9.   I know how to live without a checking account.

_____ 10.   I know how to live without electricity and a phone.

_____ 11.   I know how to use a knife as scissors.

_____ 12.   I can entertain a group of friends with my personality and my stories.

_____ 13.   I know what to do when I don't have money to pay the bills.

_____ 14.   I know how to move in half a day.

_____ 15.   I know how to get and use food stamps or an electronic card for benefits.

_____ 16.   I know where the free medical clinics are.

_____ 17.   I am very good at trading and bartering.

_____ 18.   I can get by without a car.

www.ahaprocess.com

Could you survive in middle class?

COMPLETE THE QUIZ:

Put a check by each item you know how to do.

_____1.   I know how to get my children into Little League, piano lessons, soccer, etc.

_____2.   I know how to set a table properly.

_____3.   I know which stores are most likely to carry the clothing brands my family wears.

_____4.   My children know the best name brands in clothing.

_____5.   I know how to order in a nice restaurant.

_____6.   I know how to use a credit card, checking account, and savings account—and I understand an annuity. I understand term life insurance, disability insurance, and 20/80 medical insurance policy, as well as house insurance, flood insurance, and replacement insurance.

_____7.   I talk to my children about going to college.

_____8.   I know how to get one of the best interest rates on my new-car loan.

_____9.   I understand the difference among the principal, interest, and escrow statements on my house payment.

_____10.   I know how to help my children with their homework and do not hesitate to call the school if I need additional information.

_____11.   I know how to decorate the house for the different holidays.

_____12.   I know how to get a library card.

_____13.   I know how to use most of the tools in the garage.

_____14.   I repair items in my house almost immediately when they break—or know a repair service and call it.

Could you survive in wealth?

COMPLETE THE QUIZ:

Put a check by each item you know how to do.

     1.   I can read a menu in French, English, and another language.

     2.   I have several favorite restaurants in different countries of the world.

     3.   During the holidays, I know how to hire a decorator to identify the appropriate themes and items with which to decorate the house.

     4.   I know who my preferred financial advisor, legal service, designer, domestic-employment service, and hairdresser are.

     5.   I have at least two residences that are staffed and maintained.

     6.   I know how to ensure confidentiality and loyalty from my domestic staff.

     7.   I have at least two or three "screens" that keep people whom I do not wish to see away from me.

     8.   I fly in my own plane or the company plane.

     9.   I know how to enroll my children in the preferred private schools.

     10.   I know how to host the parties that "key" people attend.

     11.   I am on the boards of at least two charities.

     12.   I know the hidden rules of the Junior League.

     13.   I support or buy the work of a particular artist.

     14.   I know how to read a corporate financial statement and analyze my own financial statements.

Hidden Rules of Economic Class

	POVERTY	MIDDLE CLASS	WEALTH
POSSESSIONS	People.	Things.	"One of a kind" objects, legacies, pedigrees.
MONEY	To be used, spent.	To be managed.	To be conserved, invested.
PERSONALITY	Is for entertainment. Sense of humor is highly valued.	Is for acquisition and stability. Achievement is highly valued.	Is for connections. Financial, political, social connections are highly valued.
SOCIAL EMPHASIS	Social inclusion of the people they like.	Emphasis is on self-governance and self-sufficiency.	Emphasis is on social exclusion.
FOOD	Key question: Did you have enough? Quantity important.	Key question: Did you like it? Quality important.	Key question: Was it presented well? Presentation important.
CLOTHING	Clothing valued for individual style and expression of personality.	Clothing valued for its quality and acceptance into the norms of middle class. Label important.	Clothing valued for its artistic sense and expression. Designer important.
TIME	Present most important. Decisions made for moment based on feelings or survival.	Future most important. Decisions made against future ramifications.	Traditions and past history most important. Decisions made partially on basis of tradition decorum.
EDUCATION	Valued and revered as abstract but not as reality. Education is about facts.	Crucial for climbing success ladder and making money.	Necessary tradition for making and maintaining connections.
DESTINY	Believes in fate. Cannot do much to mitigate chance.	Believes in choice. Can change future with good choices now.	Noblesse oblige.
LANGUAGE	Casual register. Language is about survival.	Formal register. Language is about negotiation.	Formal register. Language is about connection.
FAMILY STRUCTURE	Tends to be matriarchal.	Tends to be patriarchal.	Depends on who has/controls money.
WORLD VIEW	Sees world in terms of local setting.	Sees world in terms of national setting.	Sees world in terms of an international view.
LOVE	Love and acceptance conditional, based on whether individual is liked.	Love and acceptance conditional, based largely on achievement.	Love and acceptance conditional, related to social standing and connections.
DRIVING FORCES	Survival, relationships, entertainment.	Work and achievement.	Financial, political, social connections.

believe that one is fated or destined

↓

the behavior

↓

not get caught

↓

deny

↓

punished
forgiven

MODULE 6

DISCIPLINE INTERVENTIONS

VOICES

- Quit picking on me.
- You don't love me.
- You want me to leave.
- Nobody likes (loves) me.
- I hate you.
- You're ugly.
- You make me sick.
- It's your fault.
- Don't blame me.
- She, he, _____ did it.
- You make me mad.
- You made me do it.

- You shouldn't (should) do that.
- It's wrong (right) to do _____.
- That's stupid, immature, out of line, ridiculous.
- Life's not fair. Get busy.
- You are good, bad, worthless, beautiful (any judgmental, evaluative comment).
- You do as I say.
- If you weren't so _____, this wouldn't happen to you.
- Why can't you be like _____?

- In what ways could this be resolved?
- What factors will be used to determine the effectiveness, quality, of _____?
- I would like to recommend _____.
- What are choices in this situation?
- I am comfortable (uncomfortable) with _____.
- Options that could be considered are _____.
- For me to be comfortable, I need the following things to occur: _____.
- These are the consequences of that choice/action: _____.
- We agree to disagree.

Adapted from work of Eric Berne

www.ahaprocess.com

Working With Students From Poverty: Discipline

By Ruby K. Payne, Ph.D.
Founder and President of aha! Process, Inc.

In poverty, discipline is often about penance and forgiveness. Because love is unconditional and because the time frame is the present, the notion that discipline should be instructive and change behavior is not a part of the culture in generational poverty. In matriarchal, generational poverty, the mother is the most powerful position and is in some ways "keeper of the soul," so she dispenses the judgments, determines the amount and price of penance, and gives forgiveness. When forgiveness is granted, behaviors and activities return to the way they were before the incident.

It is important to note that the approach is to teach a separate set of behaviors. Many of the behaviors students bring to school help them survive outside of school. Students learn and use many different rules depending on the video game they are playing. Likewise, they need to learn to use different rules to be successful in the setting they are in. If poor students do not know how to fight physically, they are going to be in danger on the streets. But if that is their only method for resolving a problem, then they cannot be successful in school.

The culture of poverty does not provide for success in the middle class, because the middle class to a large extent requires the self-governance of behavior. To be successful in work and in school requires the self-governance of behavior. What then do schools need to do to teach appropriate behavior?

Structure and Choice

The two anchors of any effective discipline program that moves students to self-governance are structure and choice. The program must clearly outline the expected behaviors and the consequences of not choosing those behaviors. The program must also emphasize that the individual always has choice – to follow or not to follow the expected behaviors. With each choice then comes consequence – either desirable or not desirable. Many discipline workshops use this approach and are available to schools.

When the focus is, "I'll tell you what to do and when," the student can never move from dependence to independence. He or she is always at the level of dependence.

Behavior Analysis

Mentally or in writing, teachers or administrators must first examine the behavior analysis:

1. Decide what behaviors the child needs to have to be successful.
2. Does the child have the resources to develop those behaviors?
3. Will it help to contact a parent?

Are resources available through them? What resources are available through the school district?

4. How will behaviors be taught?
5. What are other choices the child could make?
6. What will help the child repeat the successful behavior?

When these questions are completed, they provide answers to the strategies that will most help the student. The chart on the next page indicates possible explanations of behaviors and possible interventions.

Participation of the Student

While the teacher or administrator is analyzing, the student must analyze as well. To help students do so, give them this four-part questionnaire. This has been used with students as young as second semester, first grade. Students have the most difficulty with question number three. Basically, they see no other choices available than the one they have made.

> **Name:**
> 1. **What did you do?**
> 2. **Why did you do that?**
> 3. **List four other things you could have done.**
> 4. **What will you do next time?**

In going over the sheet with the student, it is important to discuss other choices that could have been made. Students often do not have

The culture of poverty does not provide for success in the middle class, because the middle class to a large extent requires the self-governance of behavior.

Behavior Related to Poverty

Laughs when disciplined. A way to save face in matriarchal poverty.

Argues loudly with the teacher. Poverty is participatory, and the culture has a distrust of authority. Sees the system as inherently dishonest and unfair.

Angry response. Anger is based on fear. The question is what the fear is – loss of face?

Inappropriate or vulgar comments. They rely on casual register, may not know formal register.

Physically fights. Necessary to survive in poverty. Only knows the language of survival. Does not have language or belief system to use conflict resolution. Sees himself as less than a man if does not fight.

Hands always on someone else. Poverty has a heavy reliance on nonverbal data and touch.

Cannot follow directions. Little procedural memory used in poverty. Sequence not used or valued.

Extremely disorganized. Lack of planning, scheduling or prioritizing skills. Not taught in poverty. Also, probably does not have a place to put things at home so they can be found.

Only completed part of a task. No procedural self talk. Does not "see" the whole task.

Disrespectful to teacher. Has lack of respect for authority and the system. May not know any adults worthy of respect.

Harms other students, verbally or physically. This may be a way of life. Probably a way to buy space or distance. May have become a habitual response. Poverty tends to address issues in the negative.

Cheats or steals. Indicative of weak support system, weak role models/emotional resources. May indicate extreme financial need. May indicate no instruction/ guidance during formative years.

Constantly talks. Poverty is very participatory.

Intervention

Understand the reason for the behavior. Tell the student three or four other behaviors that would be more appropriate.

Don't argue with the student. Have them complete the four-part questionnaire on page 1. Model respect for students.

Respond in the adult voice. When the student cools down, discuss other responses that could be used.

Make students generate or teach students other phrases that could be used to say the same thing.

Stress that fighting is unacceptable in school. Examine other options the student could live with at school. One option is not to settle the business at school.

Allow them to draw or doodle. Have them hold their hands behind their backs when in line or standing. Give them as much to do with their hands as possible in a constructive way.

Write steps on the board. Have them write at the top of the paper the steps needed to finish the task. Have them practice procedural self-talk.

Teach a simple color-coded method of organization in the classroom. Use the five-finger method for memory at the end of the day. Make students give a plan for their own organization.

Write on the board all the parts of the task. Make students check off each part when finished.

Tell students that approach is not a choice. Identify for students the correct voice tone and word choice that is acceptable. Make them practice.

Tell the students that approach is not a choice. Have the students generate other options. Give students alternative verbal phrases.

Use metaphor story to find the reason or need the cheating and stealing met. Address the reason or need. Stress that the behavior is illegal and not a choice at school.

Make students write all questions and responses on a note card two days a week. Tell students they get five comments a day. Build participatory activities into the lesson.

access to another way to deal with the situation. For example, if I slam my finger in the car door, I can cry, cuss, hit the car, be silent, kick the tire, laugh, stoically open the car door, groan, etc.

The Language of Negotiation

One of the bigger issues with students from poverty is that many of them are their own parents. They parent themselves and others – often younger siblings. In many instances, they are the parent to the adult in the household.

Inside everyone's head are internal voices that guide the individual. These three voices are referred to as the child voice, the adult voice and the parent voice. It has been my observation that individuals who have become their own parent quite young do not have an internal adult voice. They have a child voice and a parent voice, but not an adult voice.

What an internal adult voice does is allow for negotiation. This voice provides the language of negotiation and allows the issues to be examined in a non-threatening way.

Educators tend to speak to students in a parent voice, particularly in discipline situations. To the student who is already functioning as a parent, this is unbearable, and almost immediately, the incident is exacerbated beyond the original happening. The tendency is for educators to also use the parent voice with poor parents because the assumption is that a lack of resources must indicate a lack of intelligence. Poor parents are extremely offended by this as well.

When the parent voice is used with a student who is already a parent in many ways, the outcome is anger. The student is angry because anger is based on fear. What the parent voice forces the student to do is either use the child voice or use the parent voice. If the student uses the parent voice, the student will get in trouble. If the student uses the child

> **Educators tend to speak to students in a parent voice, particularly in discipline situations. To the student who is already functioning as a parent, this is unbearable, and almost immediately, the incident is exacerbated beyond the original happening.**

voice, he or she will feel helpless and therefore at the mercy of the adult. Many students choose to use the parent voice in return because it is less frightening than the memories connected with being helpless.

Part of the reality of poverty is the language of survival. There are simply not enough resources to engage in a discussion of them. For example, if there are five hot dogs and five people, the distribution of the food is fairly clear. The condiments for the hot dogs are going to be limited so the discussion will be fairly limited as well. So the ability to see options and to negotiate among those options is not well developed. Contrast that, for example, with a middle class household where the discussion will be about how many hot dogs, what should go on the hot dog, etc.

To teach students to use the "language of negotiation," one must first teach them the phrases they can use. Especially, beginning in grade four, have them use the "adult" voice in discussions. Direct teach the notion of an adult voice and give them phrases to use. Make them tally each time they use a phrase from the "adult" voice. There will be laughter. However, over time, if teachers also model that voice in their interactions with students, they will hear more of those kinds of questions and statements.

In addition to this, several staff development programs are available to teach peer negotiation as well. It is important that as a part of the negotiation, the culture of origin is not

denigrated, but rather the ability to negotiate is seen as a survival skill for the work and school setting.

CHILD VOICE
Defensive, victimized, emotional, whining, lose mentality, strong negative non-verbal.

Quit picking on me. You don't love me. You want me to leave. Nobody likes (loves) me. I hate you. You are ugly. You make me sick. It's your fault. Don't blame me. She (he) did it. You make me mad. You made me do it.

The child voice is also playful, spontaneous, curious, etc. The phrases listed occur in conflict or manipulative situations and impede resolution.

ADULT VOICE
Non-judgmental, free of negative non-verbal, factual, often in question format, attitude of win-win.

In what ways could this be resolved? What criteria will be used to determine the effectiveness and quality of … I would like to recommend … What are the choices in this situation? I am comfortable (uncomfortable) with … Options that could be considered are … For me to be comfortable. I need the following things to occur … These are the consequences of that choice or action … We agree to disagree.

PARENT VOICE
Authoritative, directive, judgmental, evaluative, win-lose mentality, advising, (sometimes threatening, demanding, punitive).

You should not (should) do that. It is wrong (right) to do that. I would advise you to … That's stupid, immature, out of line, ridiculous. Life's not fair. Get busy. You are good, bad, worthless, beautiful (any judgmental, evaluative comment). You do as I say. If you weren't so …, this wouldn't happen to you.

The parent voice can also be very loving and supportive. These phrases listed occur during conflict and impede resolution. The internal parent voice can create shame and guilt.

Using Metaphor Stories

Another technique for working with students and adults is to use a metaphor story. A metaphor story will help an individual voice issues that affect their actions.

A metaphor story does not have any proper names in it. For example, a student keeps going to the nurse's office two or three times a week. There is nothing wrong with her, yet she keeps going.

Adult to Jennifer, the girl: "Jennifer, I am going to tell a story and I need you to help me. It is about a fourth-grade girl much like yourself. I need you to help me tell the story because I am not in the fourth grade. Once upon a time, there was a girl who went to the nurse's office. Why did the girl go to the nurse's office? *(Because she thought there was something wrong with her.)* So the girl went to the nurse's office because she thought there was something wrong with her. Did the nurse find anything wrong with her. *(No, the nurse did not.)* So the nurse did not find anything wrong with her, yet the girl kept going to the nurse. Why did the girl keep going to the nurse? *(Because she thought there was something wrong with her.)* So the girl thought something was wrong with her. Why did the girl think there was something wrong with her? *(She saw a TV show …)*"

The story continues until the reason for the behavior is found and then the story needs to end on a positive note. "So, she went to the doctor, and he gave her tests and found that she was OK."

This is an actual case. What came out in the story was that Jennifer had seen a TV show in which a girl her age had died suddenly and had never known she was ill. Jennifer's parents took her to the doctor. He ran tests and told her she was fine. She did not go to the nurse's office anymore.

A metaphor story is to be used one-on-one when there is a need to understand the behavior and what is needed is to move the student to the appropriate behavior.

Teaching Hidden Rules

For example, if a student from poverty laughs when he is disciplined, the teacher needs to say, " Do you use the same rules to play all video games: No, you don't because you would lose. The same is true at school. There are street rules and there are school rules. Each set of rules helps you be successful where you are. So, at school, laughing when disciplined is not a choice. It does not help you to be successful. It only buys you more trouble. Keep a straight face and look contrite, even if you aren't."

That is an example of teaching a hidden rule. It can even be more straight forward with older students. "Look, there are hidden rules on the street and hidden rules at school. What are they?" And then after the discussion, detail the rules that make the student successful where they are.

What Does This Information Mean in the School or Work Setting?

Students from poverty need to have at least two sets of behaviors from which to choose – one set for the streets, and one set for school and work.

The purpose of discipline should be to promote successful behaviors at school.

Teaching students to use the adult voice, i.e. the language of negotiation, is important for their success in and out of school and can become an alternative to physical aggression.

Structure and choice need to be a part of the discipline approach.

Discipline should be a form of instruction.

Previously printed in *Instructional Leader* magazine.

Ruby K. Payne, Ph.D., founder and president of **aha!** Process, Inc. (1994), with more than 30 years experience as a professional educator, has been sharing her insights about the impact of poverty – and how to help educators and other professionals work effectively with individuals from poverty – in more than a thousand workshop settings through North America, Canada, and Australia.

More information on her book, *A Framework for Understanding Poverty*, can be found on her website, www.ahaprocess.com.

Editor's note: Dr. Ruby Payne produced *Preventing School Violence by Creating Emotional Safety*, a 5-part video series and manual which is often used as part of teacher orientation.

Dr. Payne also presents these ideas in depth in *A Framework for Understanding Poverty*, a two-day workshop, on her U.S. National Tour each year. This video series and National Tour dates are available on her website, www.ahaprocess.com. We invite you to opt-in to **aha!**'s e-mail newslist for the latest poverty and income statistics [free] and other updates.

aha! Process, Inc.
(800) 424-9484
(281) 426-5300
fax: (281) 426-5600
www.ahaprocess.com

> ## Students from poverty need to have at least two sets of behaviors from which to choose— one set for the streets, and one set for school and work.

MODULE 7

BUILDING RELATIONSHIPS

creating relationships

DEPOSITS	WITHDRAWALS
Seeking first to understand	Seeking first to be understood
Keeping promises	Breaking promises
Kindnesses, courtesies	Unkindnesses, discourtesies
Clarifying expectations	Violating expectations
Loyalty to the absent	Disloyalty, duplicity
Apologies	Pride, conceit, arrogance
Open to feedback	Rejecting feedback

Adapted from The Seven Habits of Highly Effective People *by Stephen Covey*

DEPOSITS MADE TO INDIVIDUAL IN POVERTY	WITHDRAWALS MADE FROM INDIVIDUAL IN POVERTY
Appreciation for humor and entertainment provided by the individual	Put-downs or sarcasm about the humor or the individual
Acceptance of what the individual cannot say about a person or situation	Insistence and demands for full explanation about a person or situation
Respect for the demands and priorities of relationships	Insistence on the middle-class view of relationships
Using the adult voice	Using the parent voice
Assisting with goal-setting	Telling the individual his/her goals
Identifying options related to available resources	Making judgments on the value and availability of resources
Understanding the importance of personal freedom, speech, and individual personality	Assigning pejorative character traits to the individual

www.ahaprocess.com

What can a teacher do to build relationships?

TESA (Teacher Expectations and Student Achievement) identified 15 behaviors that teachers use with good students.

The research study found that when teachers used these interactions with low-achieving students, their achievement made significant gains.

1. Calls on everyone in the room equitably

2. Provides individual help

3. Gives "wait" time (allows student enough time to answer)

4. Asks questions to give the student clues about the answer

5. Asks questions that require more thought

6. Tells students whether their answers are right or wrong

7. Gives specific praise

8. Gives reasons for praise

9. Listens

10. Accepts feelings of the student

11. Gets within an arm's reach of each student each day

12. Is courteous to students

13. Shows personal interest and gives compliments

14. Touches students (appropriately)

15. Desists (he or she does not call attention to every negative behavior)

Source: TESA (Teacher Expectation and Student Achievement), Los Angeles Department of Education

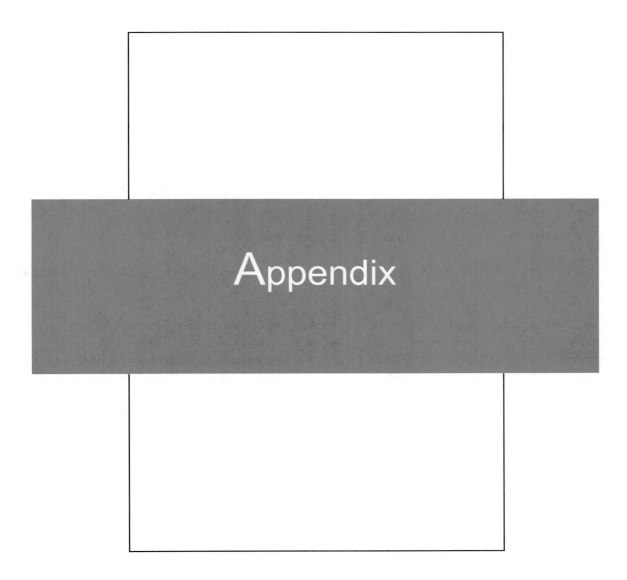

Appendix

WORKING WITH STUDENTS' PARENTS AND GUARDIANS

Do not confuse having physical presence with parental involvement. The research seems to indicate that when a parent provides *support, insistence, and expectations* to the child, the presence or absence of a parent in the physical school building is immaterial. Therefore, training for parents should concentrate on these issues.

Think of parents not as a single group but as distinct sub-groups. For example:

   1) career-oriented/too busy to attend school activities

   2) very involved in school activities

   3) single parents working two jobs/too busy to attend

   4) immigrant parents with language issues

   5) parents with overwhelming personal issues, such as addiction, illness, incarceration, evading the law

   6) surrogate parents: foster parents, grandparents, et al.

   7) children who, in effect, are their own parents; they no longer have involved parents or guardians.

In your campus plan, identify specific ways you will target each group. Many discipline problems come from students whose parents are in sub-groups 5 and 7. These students desperately need relationships with adults that are long-term and stable. As a rule of thumb, the best (only?) way to make contact with groups 5 and 6 is through home visits, when and where possible. In sub-groups 5 and 7, the children/teens themselves are the *de facto* parents. Often they work full time in order to provide enough money for both the children *and* adults to survive. Time is a key issue for those students. *It is unrealistic to treat parents as one group. The needs and issues are very different.*

TIPS FOR WORKING WITH STUDENTS' PARENTS AND GUARDIANS

- Phone systems: Let parents and guardians talk to a real person. Phone systems at secondary schools often make it very difficult to talk to anyone.

- Have an awards assembly for parents.

- Identify a clear mechanism for getting information. For affluent parents, a Website is wonderful. For all parents, videos work. The videos need to be short and focused. For example, how to talk to your teenager, how to find out what is happening at the high school, how to get your child back to school after a suspension, etc.

 www.ahaprocess.com

- Another option is a predictable newsletter. But it needs to be simple, clear, and to the point—and it must include many icons or visuals so that it can be used whether you're literate or extremely busy. These newsletters can be posted outside the building in glass cases and updated weekly. They can be posted in supermarkets, Laundromats, etc. The National Honor Society could take it on as a service project. Newsletters can be mailed home, a better option than children carrying them home.

- Pay parents to come in and call other parents. Have a list of things to say and have two rules: You may not discuss teachers and you may not discuss students other than your own children.

- Have gatherings that involve *food*. For example, anyone can come to the school for 50-cent hot dogs.

- If you do parenting classes, don't call them that. Focus on the student: "How to help your child …" Many parents of teenagers are desperate for good information about teens. Teenagers are typically tight-lipped and, unless you have much opportunity to be around them, as a parent you may not even know what is "normal." Find ways for individuals with lots of exposure to teenagers to share that information with parents and guardians.

- Adopt a plot of land to keep landscaped and clean. One school in a very poor neighborhood did this. Parents took pride in it. (Some even planted tomatoes!)

- Divide parents up among all the staff members (secretaries included). Each staff member contacts those parents and tells them, "If you have a question you cannot get an answer to, you can always call me."

- Create emotional safety for parents by being respectful of their concerns, openly sharing school activities, clarifying behavioral parameters/expectations of the school, and identifying available opportunities.

- For all activities, organizations, handbooks, etc., use simpler formats for giving the information. Liberally use visuals to appeal to the illiterate, the immigrant, and the busy.

WORKING WITH PARENTS FROM POVERTY

The first issue to address when working with parents from poverty is mutual respect. The second is the use of casual register. The third is the way discipline is used in the household. The fourth is the way time is viewed. And the fifth is the role of school and education in their lives.

First, for many parents in generational poverty, school is not given a high priority. It is often feared and resented. Their own personal experience may not have been positive, and school is alternately viewed as a babysitter or a necessary evil (i.e., "If I don't send my child, I will have to go to court"). Second, when parents come in, because of their heavy reliance on a win/lose approach to conflict, they may begin with an in-your-face approach. Remember, they are doing this, consciously or unconsciously, as a show of strength. Just stay in the adult voice. Use language that is clear and straightforward. If you use "educationese," they're likely to think you're trying to cheat or trick them.

Use these kinds of phrases with parents from poverty (these are the types of comments they often use with their own children):

- "Learning this will help your child win more often."

- "The mind is a mental weapon that no one can take from you."

- "If you do this, your child will be smarter and won't get cheated or tricked."

- "Learning this will help your child make more money."

- "This information will help keep your child safer."

- "I know you love and care about your child very much or you wouldn't be here" (but don't say this if you don't mean it).

Discipline in generational poverty vacillates from being very permissive to very punitive. The emotional mood of the moment often determines what occurs. Also, in some cultures, the approach to boys is very different from the approach to girls. When the discipline is highly punitive, there is often a belief system that (a) the harsher the punishment, the greater the forgiveness, and (b) the harsher punishment will make the young person stronger and tougher. Consequently, the notion of a systematic approach to discipline usually doesn't exist. There is rarely mediation or intervention about a behavior. Generally, it is a slap and a "Quit that." If guidance is being provided to the parent about behavior, use a WHAT, WHY, HOW approach with visuals. (See Ruby's comments at the end of this section on page 70, as well as a visual example of WHAT, WHY, HOW on page 71)

GETTING PARENTS FROM POVERTY TO COME TO THE SCHOOL SETTING

One of the big difficulties for many schools is simply getting the parents into the school setting. Howard Johnson, a researcher at Southern Florida University, has done work with why urban parents come to school. The first reason they usually come is a crisis. What he has found is that rarely do they come to the school for reasons that school people think are important. So the first question that must be asked when trying to get parents to school is: "What's in it for the parents?"

A study done by the U.S. government in 1993 with Chapter 1 schools looked only at schools that were 75% or more low-income. Administrators of the study then identified students within those schools who achieved and students who did not. They developed a questionnaire looking at criteria in and out of school to understand the variables that made a difference in achievement. Interestingly, whether parents actually went to school or attended meetings at school was not a significant factor. What made the biggest difference was whether or not parents provided these three things for their children: *support, insistence, and expectations*.

SOME SUGGESTIONS (WHEN PARENTS FROM POVERTY COME TO THE SCHOOL)

1) Rather than the meeting format, *use the museum format*. That way parents can come and go when it's convenient for their schedule and their inclination. In other words, the school would be open from 6 to 9 p.m. Parents could come to one room to watch a video or a student performance. These would be repeated every 20 to 30 minutes. Another room could have a formal meeting at a given time. Another room could have board games for the students. Another room could have food.

2) *Have food*. Give gift certificates to grocery stores. These tend to be popular. Another favorite is clothesbaskets that have soap, shampoo, perfumes, etc., since food stamps don't always allow those purchases.

3) *Let the children come with the parents*—for several reasons. First, there often is jealousy or suspicion by the husband when his wife goes out alone. If the woman's children are with her, there is none. Second, school buildings tend to be big and confusing to parents. If the children go with them, the children help them find their way around. Third, a babysitter frequently isn't available. And fourth, children are natural icebreakers. Parents meet each other through their children.

4) *Have classes that benefit parents*. For example: how to speak English; how to fill out a job application; how to get a Social Security card; how to make money mowing yards, doing child care, baking, and repairing small engines. Also, schools can make their computer labs available on Saturdays to teach things like CAD (computer-aided design) and word processing—simple introductory courses that last four to five Saturdays for a couple of hours.

ALTERNATIVE APPROACHES

1) Use video. Virtually every home in poverty has a TV and a VCR or DVD player, even if it has very little else. Keep the videos under 15 minutes.

2) For all fliers home, use both verbal *and* visual information.

3) Provide simple, how-to activities that parents can do with children.

TIPS FOR WORKING WITH PARENTS FROM POVERTY

- Many adults from poverty didn't have a positive school experience. The greeting of the first staff member they encounter (secretary, aide, administrator, teacher) will either confirm their earlier experience or counter it. Some sort of building procedure and greeting should be agreed upon.

- Always call them by Mr. or Mrs. (unless told otherwise). It's a sign of respect.

- Identify your intent. Intent determines non-verbals. Parents from poverty decide if they like you based largely on your non-verbals. If they don't like you, they won't support you or work with you. For example, if your intent is to win, that will be reflected in your non-verbals. Likewise, if your intent is to understand, that will be reflected as well.

- Use humor (not sarcasm). They particularly look to see if you have a sense of humor about yourself. For example: Can you tell a story about yourself in which you weren't the hero? Can you poke fun at yourself?

- Deliver bad news through a story. If you state the bad news directly (e.g., your son was stealing), it will invite an automatic defense of the child. Instead, say, "Let me tell you a story. Maybe you can help me with the situation." Make sure you use the word *story*.

- If you're comfortable using casual register, use it. If not, don't use it. They'll probably think you're making fun of them.

- Be human and don't be afraid to indicate you don't have all the answers. As alluded to above, they distrust anyone who is "always the hero of his/her stories."

- Offer a cup of coffee. In poverty, coffee is frequently offered as a sign of welcome.

- Use the adult voice. Be understanding but firm. Be open to discussion, but don't change the consequences (unless new information surfaces or a better solution can be found).

- Be personally strong. You aren't respected in generational poverty unless you are personally strong. If you're threatened or have an in-your-face encounter, don't show fear. You don't need to be mean. Just don't show fear.

- If they're angry, they may appeal to physical power ("I'm going to beat you up!"). To calm them, say, "I know you love and care about your child very much or you wouldn't be here. What can we do that would show we also care?" Another phrase that often works is: "Are you mad at me, or are you just mad?"

- Use videos as a way to provide information and communicate with parents. Virtually every U.S. home in poverty has a TV, VCR, and DVD player. If possible, make the videos entertaining. They can be in any language, but they should be short.

- Story structure in generational poverty is episodic and random, and the discourse pattern is circular. Understand that these structures take much longer. Allow enough time during conferences for these structures to be used.

- *Home visits by teachers are the fastest and easiest way to build a huge parent support base quickly.* They also significantly reduce discipline issues. Use Title I money to pay teachers to make phone calls and do home visits before there is a problem. (The payoff from this one simple activity is tremendous.)

- Remember, the parents from poverty talked about you in the neighborhood before they came to see you. They often made outrageous comments about what they were going to say and do to you before they went to the school (entertainment is an important part of the culture of poverty). So when they return to the neighborhood, they have to report back. Some comments you may end up hearing will be so outrageous that they should be ignored. They were made because they told people in the neighborhood they were going to do so.

- As you discuss situations with parents, ask yourself what resources are available to these individuals. Some suggestions won't work because the resources simply aren't available.

- In middle class, when a topic is introduced that the individual doesn't want to discuss, he/she simply changes the subject. In generational poverty, the individual often tells the person what he/she wants to hear, particularly if that person is in a position of authority.

- Emphasize that there are two sets of rules: one set for school and work, another set for outside of school and work.

- Don't accept behaviors from adults that you don't accept from students.

TIPS FOR WORKING WITH PARENTS FROM WEALTH

- Don't use humor—at least initially—when discussing their child or situation. If you do, they'll think you don't care about them or their child.

- One of the hidden rules in affluence is: "It's not OK not to be perfect." So identifying your personal weaknesses will not appeal to them particularly. They want to know that you are very good at what you do. On the other hand, if you don't know something, don't try to bluff your way through. They will usually call your bluff.

- Another hidden rule in affluence is that you aren't respected unless you're able to discriminate by quality or artistic merit. Wealthy parents won't respect you unless you have expertise. In you aren't knowledgeable in a particular area, read the experts or get a school district expert to sit in with you for the meeting.

- Don't use circular discourse or casual register. They want to get straight to the point and discuss the issue through formal register. They won' respect you if you waste their time.

- Do use the adult voice with affluent parents. Understand that they are skilled negotiators. Clearly establish parameters when discussing issues with them. Affluent parents often believe that they and their children don't need to follow or adhere to the "rules" of the organization. Be firm about those boundaries.

- Emphasize issues of safety, legal parameters, and the need for the student to develop coping mechanisms for greater success later in life.

- Understand that a primary motivator for wealthy parents is the financial, social, and academic success of their child. They're very interested in what you'll be able to do to help their child be successful.

- When affluent parents come to school and are upset, they likely will appeal to positional power, financial power, or connections ("I know the school board president" … "I'll call my lawyer" …). They also will attack the issues. Be prepared to articulate the issues, and use experts by name in the discussion.

- Don't be intimidated by the affluent parent. Do understand, regardless of your position, who is standing behind you to support you. If you have little or no support above you, make sure you don' paint yourself into a corner. Affluent parents will rattle the organizational "cage" in order to get what they want.

- Understand the competitive nature of wealth (especially among those with "new money") and the need to excel. Their children are expected to be the best. There tends to be disrespect for those in the service sector, including public service. However, if their child is happy and doing well, most of them will be incredibly supportive.

WORKING WITH PARENTS

OVERPROTECTIVE PARENTS

What is driving the protectiveness?

a. Child is a possession—defend your own no matter what they do.
b. Child is proof of parenting success—it's not OK not to be perfect.
c. Fear of loss—death ,affection, loyalty.
d. Loss of another child—want to protect this child.
e. Change personal experience—"My mother never loved me."
f. Beliefs about parenting—"I just want to love him or her."
g. Emotional need of parent—loneliness, co-dependence, addiction.

Questions to ask

a. What is the very worst thing that could happen if we … ?
b. What is the very best thing that could happen if we … ?
c. What coping strategies could your child learn so that he or she could be more successful?
d. I know you love and care about your child very much. What can we do so that you know we love and care about him or her too?
e. Is there any evidence the fear is a reality?
f. How will this request help your child be more successful?
g. At what age will you allow your child to be responsible for his or her own actions?

Interventions

a. Reframing.
b. Using a story.
c. Establishing the parameters of school success.
d. Using other parents to establish perspective.
e. Establishing the parameters of parental interventions at school.

Appeals

Among affluent parents, an appeal to one of the following is effective: safety, expertise, legalities, or coping strategies to be more successful.

Among parents from poverty, an appeal to caring, winning, being smarter, or not getting cheated is effective.

CONFERENCING WITH PARENTS

A PROCESS

1. Stop the blackmail (if that is a part of the conference).

2. Listen. If needed, ask the parent to repeat the conversation and say this, "I am going to put this in writing and I want you to read back over it to see if I have gotten the main concerns. I will share this with the teacher and begin to work on this issue."

3. Pivot the conversation. Find out what the parent wants.
    "Are you just mad or are you mad at me?"
    "If you were queen or king, what would be your ideal solution to this?"

4. Establish the parameters, i.e. what the limitations of the situation are. (In some cases, you must get back with the parents after you have had a chance to find out the legal ramifications.)

5. Discuss options within those parameters.

6. Identify solutions.

7. Identify a plan. If necessary, put the plan in writing.

CASE STUDY: ANDREA

Andrea is a senior in high school. The counselor has come to you with a concern. It is the third six weeks of the first semester and Andrea is failing Algebra II honors. Andrea needs Algebra II to graduate. You call the parent in to look at the possibility of Andrea taking regular Algebra II so that she can get the credit and graduate. Algebra II is not offered as a part of summer school.

Andrea's mother comes in for the conference. She informs you in no uncertain terms that Andrea will not switch to an Algebra II regular class. Andrea is going to go to Texas A&M, all her friends are in that class, and she will not be switching. You explain to the mother that she will not have a diploma if she does not get a credit in Algebra II and that without a diploma she will not be admitted into A&M. The mother indicates that Andrea's grades are not the issue. Andrea's friends are the issue, and she is not going to approve the change.

- What is driving the parent behavior?

- What questions would you ask the parent?

- What intervention(s) would you make?

CASE STUDY: ANDY SLOCUM

Andy is in fourth grade. He is one of the youngest students in his class because he was barely 5 in first grade. You like Andy. Mrs. Slocum, his mother, is always at school. The family is very affluent, and Andy is her only child. The gossip network has it that Mrs. Slocum was married before and had two children and lost them in a custody battle.

Mrs. Slocum comes to you in March and tells you that she wants to retain Andy in the fourth grade. She knows he is gifted, but his grades aren't high enough to be in the program. He has been making A's and B's. She wants him to have all A's. From your observations, Andy is a bright child, he is somewhat immature (in comparison to his classmates), but he is very likable, has a winning personality, and is athletically gifted.

You tell Mrs. Slocum about the research regarding retention. The counselor has a conversation with Andy. You talk to the teacher about Mrs. Slocum request, and the teacher is appalled. You tell Mrs. Slocum that you will not recommend retention. She tells you she will go to the superintendent if you don't recommend retention.

- What is driving the parent behavior?

- What questions would you ask the parent?

- What intervention(s) would you make?

CASE STUDY: CHARLES

You have a school that is 95% low-income, and at the fifth-grade level you have instituted a decision-making unit. Charles is in fifth grade, and his mother calls you one day and says the following:

"I heard that school was teaching decision making. My son ain't learnin' it. I want you to tell him that he has got to quit stealing so close to home. He needs to go three or four streets over. I don't know what that boy's problem is. That ain't no kind of decision making. If he can't make better decisions, I'm gonna tell the neighborhood about how your school ain't no good. And why they spendin' all that time on makin' decisions when he still don't know how to add?"

- What is driving the parent behavior?

- What questions would you ask the parent?

- What intervention(s) would you make?

CASE STUDY: MICHAEL

You are walking back to your office after visiting classrooms, and Mrs. Walker comes running in the front door. "What is wrong with Michael?" she asks. Michael is her son who's in third grade.

You say, "I haven't seen Michael this morning."

"Well, he just called and said that there is a problem. I need to talk to him."

Michael is called down to the office. During the conversation with his mother, it becomes apparent that Michael is angry with his teacher. He asked to get a drink of water, and instead went to the pay phone, called his mother, and told her to get up there right now. He's angry with his teacher because she gave an assignment he didn't want to do.

- What is driving the parent behavior?

- What questions would you ask the parent?

- What intervention(s) would you make?

CASE STUDY: MRS. SMITH

Mrs. Smith is a loud, gossiping parent who is active in the PTO. She has a son and a daughter. The son receives the focus of her attention. Yesterday Mrs. Smith called you because she is furious with you. She wants to know why you didn't do something about those students who put her fifth-grade son, Sam, in the trashcan at lunch. She tells you that if you don't do something about it, she will send her husband up there to "get you."

You aren't as concerned about that as you are that Mrs. Smith will go to the superintendent again with a badly skewed story.

You are surprised. The aides in the lunchroom are excellent, and you haven't heard anything about anyone being put in a trashcan. You talk to the fifth-grade teachers and the aides. No one heard anything about this, nor did they see anything.

So you call Sam in and talk to him. You ask for details about the incident—when, where, who. The details are very fuzzy: No, it wasn't during lunch, it was in the hall. He couldn't remember the names; they stuffed him in there before he could see them.

You probe some more. Finally, Sam says, "Every night when I go home my mom asks me what bad thing happened at school today. If I say nothing, she tells me I'm lying to her. So I decided to tell her I got put in a trashcan."

You recall incident after incident where Mom "rescues" Sam and threatens to send Dad up to see you if you don't do what she wants.

- What is driving the parent behavior?

- What questions would you ask the parent?

- What intervention(s) would you make?

CASE STUDY: MR. AND MRS. DESHOTELS

The second-grade teacher comes to you in January and tells you that Jacque has already had 25 absences this school year. The teacher has called Jacque's mother for an explanation, but the only explanation is that Jacque doesn't feel well. You look at her records for the year before; she had 36 absences in first grade.

You call the home and are unable to make contact. You get an answering machine. Finally, you send a letter, outlining the law about absences and stating your concern. You hear nothing. The next week, Jacque is absent another two days. You send a letter requesting a conference and indicate that if the absences continue without explanation, you will be required to take the next legal step.

You get a phone call from Mr. Deshotels. He cusses at you, tells you he will get a lawyer, etc. You find out from his monologue that he is a long-distance trucker, and you ask him if he knows how many absences his daughter has. He replies belligerently that he does. You say that you think 26 absences without a medical cause for one semester are excessive. Suddenly there is silence at the other end of the phone.

- What is driving the parent behavior?

- What questions would you ask the parent?

- What intervention(s) would you make?

CASE STUDY: MRS. BROWN

Mrs. Brown is a member of the Pentecostal Church, and she comes to see you about a novel that is being used in fourth grade. She is *very* upset that the school would have this book. The book is about a 12-year-old boy who goes on a hunt for a deer and comes to understand who he is. It's a book about coming of age and finding identity. She explains to you that the book is really not about a hunt, but the deer really represents a female and the book is about the sexual hunt. You tell her that the district has a choice option on books and that her daughter does not need to read the book; another book will be found for her daughter.

Mrs. Brown isn't satisfied and tells you that you don't understand. The book isn't suitable for any fourth-grader, says Mrs. Brown, and she will work long and hard to make sure it isn't read by anyone in fourth grade, adding that it's wrong to have a book like that in the schools. She has talked to her minister about it. Her minister is willing to go to a board meeting with her to protest the use of such inappropriate sexual reading in elementary school.

- What is driving the parent behavior?

- What questions would you ask the parent?

- What intervention(s) would you make?

A NOTE RUBY PAYNE RECEIVED FROM AN ASSISTANT PRINCIPAL

I attended the Train the Trainers session in Houston in July. It was great. At the time, I had no idea how useful it was going to be when I was placed as assistant principal for the first time.

I am having a hard time in this school because there is a problem I've never had to deal with. It sounds like something Ruby could shed some light on, but I don't remember her covering it at the session. A large number of parents in this school *beat* their children when I send a note or call home about the students' behaviors. I have had to call [child protective services] many days after punishing a child. Staff members at school are as overwhelmed as I am. They say this hasn't been a large problem until just recently. Many are holding back on sending students to the office because of fear of how the parents will handle the child afterward. All of us are anxious for some guidance. Can you give us some information or recommend some sources where we can do some reading? We pray for both Ruby and divine guidance. You can e-mail me here at school or at home.

RUBY'S RESPONSE

It was great to hear from you and know that the training was helpful.

About beating children. Yes, this is a very common response in generational poverty, particularly in Caucasian and African-American settings. It is not as much of a pattern in Hispanic generational poverty, unless there are multiple relationships.

There are several reasons why parents beat their children.

First, many times the parents have only two voices—a parent voice and a child voice. To move a child to self-governance, a person needs to have a third voice, an adult voice, so that the child can examine choices. Many parents cannot do this because they don't have an adult voice. So they use the parent voice. And in conflict, the parent voice tends to be a very harsh, punitive voice.

The second reason they beat their children is that typically they don't know any other approach. Usually raised themselves under punitive parenting, they believe the maxim that to spare the rod is to spoil the child.

The third reason is that it's part of the penance-forgiveness ritual. If you believe that you are fated, then you really cannot change your behavior. So the greater the penance, the greater the forgiveness. You will often find that after parents beat their children (penance) they engage in a ritual of forgiveness. Forgiveness can include any or all of the following: cooking them their favorite meal; permissiveness; and giving them alcohol, cigarettes, part of the drug stash, and money. Or a parent might even come to school and chew someone out just to show their child that he/she is forgiven. The thinking tends to be the following:

- I do the behavior because I am fated; I cannot change who I am.

- If I am fated, then I can't really change what I do.

- If I can't change what I do, then the real crime is getting caught.

- But if I get caught, then I am going to deny it.

- Because if I deny it, I might not get punished.

- However, if I do get punished, then I have also gotten forgiven.

- And I'm free to do the behavior again.

I have some suggestions for you.

First of all, I would approach the situation differently. When an incident occurs, I would call the parent and say, "I need your help. We are asking that you use a WHAT, WHY, HOW approach to discipline, which will help us here at school. That is what we are doing. When your child does something you don't like, please tell him WHAT he did, WHY that was not OK, and HOW to do it right. *We want him to win every time and be smarter at school.* So to help us, please use the WHAT, WHY, HOW approach. (As a reference point for yourself and parents, make a little brochure or paper with this approach clearly shown.) Then say, "Please do not hit him. When you hit him, we are required by law to call [child protective services]. We don't want to have to do that. So please help us."

Parents do what they believe to be the right thing. Some will say to you, "Honey, you do what you have to at school, and we'll do what we have to at home."

Then you say, "I know you love and care about your child very much or you wouldn't be taking the time to talk to me. But I need your help, and I know you don't want me to call [child protective services]. So, for anything having to do with your child and school, please use the WHAT, WHY, HOW approach. It's a simple 1-2-3 deal. It's not easy being a parent, and we want you to be able to *win* as a parent. So please help us."

For the parents with whom this doesn't work, I would not call home or send notes anymore. I would look more for positive reinforcements than negative reinforcements. There is nothing we can do at school that is as negative as some of the stuff that happens outside of school.

Please stay in touch, and let me know how things are going.

TO DISCIPLINE YOUR CHILD/STUDENT, USE THESE STEPS

1) **STOP** the behavior that is inappropriate.

2) Tell the child **WHAT** he/she did that was wrong.

3) Tell the child **WHY** the behavior was wrong and its consequences.

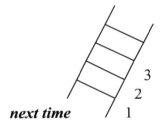

4) Tell the child **HOW** to behave the next time.

No Child Left Behind:
Parent and Community Involvement

By Ruby K. Payne, Ph.D.
*Founder and President of **aha!** Process, Inc.*
Part IV of a four-part series

An integral part of a principal's role is working with parents. Conflicts that arise because of time constraints, differing belief systems, and difficult social and behavioral issues consume a large chunk of a principal's time. Furthermore, in almost all legislation, parental involvement is now either required or considered to be a key component in improving student achievement. So how does a principal get parental involvement?

First of all, some concepts need to be revisited. There is no correlation between the *physical presence* of parents at school and student achievement. The correlation is between student achievement and *parental involvement.* So getting parents to physically come to the school is not a key issue in student achievement.

Second, another concept that needs to be revisited is the "one size fits all" approach, which only works when the student population is very homogenous. It doesn't work when the student population is racially or socioeconomically diverse.

The third concept is that our current scheduling of parental activities is fine—and that all activities must involve the parent coming in to the school. The scheduling and structuring of parental outreach and activities is often set up for the convenience of school personnel, rather than the parents, and is one-way, i.e., school personnel do not go to the parents. That needs to change.

The fourth concept is that parents actually have a support system that allows them to participate in school activities and that their experience with school has been positive. For many parents this is simply not true.

And last but not least, a concept among school personnel is that many parents are difficult. Tools to address difficult parents give teachers and administrators more efficacy and, therefore, often more success.

New Model to Involve Parents
This article is going to provide a model that involves the following: (1) niche marketing to parents; (2) building a layered, "community of support" approach (Wehlage, et al., 1989; El Puente Project, 2003) involving myriad interventions and different scheduling; and (3) tools for dealing with difficult parents, parents from different economic classes, and parent/teacher conferences.

PART I: NICHE MARKETING TO PARENTS

Niche marketing is a term used in advertising. Simply put, it means that one size does not fit all and that marketing needs to be targeted at specific audiences. The following table outlines some of the subgroups of parents found in many schools and ideas for involvement in their child's education. *A parent does not need to come to school to be involved.*

Put these activities into the site-based plan so that they occur. The activities actually become a marketing plan for the campus.

SUBGROUPS OF PARENTS	IDEAS FOR INVOLVEMENT
Two-career parents	Put many things in print, e.g., fliers, newsletters, Web pages, etc. These parents will read and keep informed. Ask for e-mail addresses and send a monthly or weekly e-mail that updates them on the classroom and school activities.
Involved parents	These parents are at school, volunteering their help. The issue here is over involvement and parents wanting to take on administrative roles. Sometimes the boundaries involving student privacy need to be revisited.
Non-working and uninvolved parents	This occurs at both ends of the economic spectrum. Phone banks where parents call parents and tell them about school activities begins a network. Home contacts are very powerful, as are coffee klatches (see Part II for explanation).
Surrogate parents	These are grandparents, foster parents, etc. They often need emotional support. Assign them a mentor—e.g., a counselor or involved parent—who touches base with them once a month.

(Chart continues on page 2)

PART I: NICHE MARKETING TO PARENTS *(continued from page 1)*

SUBGROUPS OF PARENTS	IDEAS FOR INVOLVEMENT
Immigrant parents	Make short videos dubbed in their own language explaining how school works, how to talk to the teacher, what grades mean, what homework means, etc. Have the videos made by a person in your community from that immigrant group. DO NOT MAKE THEM TOO SLICK OR PROFESSIONAL because they will not be believed.
Parents working two jobs	Color-code the information you send home. White paper is "nice to know." Yellow paper indicates a concern. Red paper means that immediate attention is needed. You can call these parents at work as long as you do not talk at that time; ask them to call you back. Videos to introduce the teacher work well also.
Single parents	Structure activities that make life easier for the parent, activities that would include the children or child care, food (so they don't need to cook), or activities scheduled on the weekends or with open time frames rather than specific meeting times. Videos to introduce the teacher also work well here.
Parents who are unavailable and students who, in effect, are their own parents	These are parents who are incarcerated, mentally ill, physically ill, traveling a great deal, have been sent back to their native country, have an addiction, etc. Teach the student how to be his/her own parent and provide linkages for the student to other school service agencies. Have the counselor have "what if" lunches where pizza is brought in and four or five students in this position discuss issues.
Parents who are "crazymakers"	There are only a few of these in a building (less than 1%), but they can destroy time and energy. These are the parents who constantly have a complaint. Each time a solution is reached, there is a new complaint. School personnel need to take their daily rate, divide it by 8 to calculate an hourly rate, and document the cost of personnel time used by one parent. No board of education wants to know that one parent took $60,000 to $70,000 of personnel time for no reason.

A part of site-based planning is to identify the percentages of parents who fit into these categories. If you have many parents in one subgroup, then it would be important to address more of those involvement issues.

PART II: BUILDING COMMUNITIES OF SUPPORT

The layering and structuring of "practices that contribute to student engagement and high school completion" is the basic concept in communities of support. "Chief among these is the ability of school personnel to create communities of support that are concerned about how students perform and express that concern in genuine, effective, caring ways" (El Puente Project, 2003). So how does one do that? One way is to create a scaffolding of interventions. The other is by creating linkages to community groups.

The following suggestions can help create communities of support for parents:

a) Mutual respect: Parents are welcomed by first-line staff. Parents are welcome in the building. Accusatory and blaming language is not present.

b) School design teams: A cross-section of staff, parents, law enforcement, ministers, and students who identify issues of support.

c) Home contacts: These are not home visits but quick five-minute visits to the home at the beginning of school to say hello. Substitutes are used to release teachers to do this.

d) Videos: These can be made by the staff and students to introduce faculty, to tell about school discipline programs, to highlight upcoming events, etc.

e) Student and parent voices: Through informal conversation (not meetings), parents and students are asked what the school could do to better serve them.

f) Weekend activities: Friday evenings, Saturday mornings, and Sunday afternoons work the best.

g) Varied and targeted parental involvement activities: Free donuts for dads the first Monday of every month. Carnations for moms. Lunch for grandparents. Picnics for people who live in the student's house.

h) Support mechanisms for parents that involve follow-up: 3x5 cards with the steps that will be followed. Magnets for the refrigerator that list school phone numbers and holidays. Stickers that parents can give to the child for good behaviors.

i) Informal coffee klatches: Counselor or principal asks a parent with whom they already have a relationship to invite three or four other friends over for coffee in the parent's home. The principal or counselor brings the donuts. This is a forum for an informal discussion about what bothers parents, what they would like to see, what they like, etc.

j) Overcoming reluctance to participate by creating one-on-one relationships.

k) Tools for dealing with
parent/teacher conferences.

l) Tools for dealing with difficult
parents.

m) Simple written documents that
have pictures and words and/or
cartoons.

n) Using networking capabilities in
the community: Make a flier with
cartoons that is one page and has
an advertisement for a business in
the community on the back.
Introduce your faculty through
cartoons. The advertiser pays for
the paper and the printing.
Distribute them to beauty salons,
grocery stores, barbershops, churches,
etc., much like a local community
shopper or merchandiser.

o) Information for parents that
enhances their lives: Offer information like how to fix bad credit
(knowledge about money), how to
manage a difficult boss (conflict-
resolution skills), etc.

p) Information on video or in cartoon
that helps parents deal with their
children, i.e., how to enhance
obedience in your child.

q) Giving awards to parents: A child
identifies something a parent has
done. On a Saturday morning the
child gives a certificate to his/her
parent and thanks the parent.

r) Parent/teacher conferences led by
the student.

s) Weekend activities that use the
computers and athletic facilities of
the campus.

t) Partner with a campus that has a
surplus of parent involvement.

u) Peer-mediation training for students:
They teach it to parents informally.

v) Teaching students to be better
friends: Have students list the five
friends they go to when they have
a problem. Tally who are the "best
friends." Teach them how to ask
questions to solve problems. Teach
them how to identify which problems
are serious and need to be
referred, such as threats of suicide.

w) Teaching parents to be better
friends to other adults.

x) Block parties: Get a street blocked
off for an afternoon and have a
party.

In other words, creating communities of support is a layered, varied set
of interventions and activities. The
idea that a school can have X number
of meetings a year, a carnival, and a
Halloween party is not enough. What
must occur is a scaffolding of interventions.

PART III: TOOLS TO USE FOR PARENT/TEACHER CONFERENCES AND DEALING WITH DIFFICULT PARENTS

School personnel need to hone their
conferencing skills to create a supportive environment for parents and
develop conflict-resolution skills to
deal more effectively with difficult
parents. Our online questionnaires for
new teachers have found that their
two greatest issues are student discipline and dealing with parents.

Outlined below is a parent/teacher
conferencing form, a step sheet for
the process to be used as a part of
parent/teacher conferences, phrases
to use by economic group, and questions to ask to facilitate resolution of
conflicts.

Step Sheet for Parent/Teacher Conferences

1. Contact the parent. If it's going to
be a difficult conference, have the
principal or a counselor attend.

2. Make a list of items that need to
be in the folder that is shared with
parents: student work, grades, discipline referrals, rubrics, tests, etc.

3. If time is short, let the parent know
about that and apologize for the
time frame.

4. Have mutual respect for the parent.
Ask the parent to tell you about
his/her child. "As we begin this
conversation, what would you like
me to know about Johnny? You
love him and care about him or
you would not have come to see
me." They know more about the
child than you do. Tap into that
knowledge. Do not use "why"
questions. Say "our child." (See
below for questions to ask.)

5. Keep the conference focused on
the data and the issues. "I have a
folder of John's work. I would like
to go through the folder with you
and talk about his work." Or, if the
student is there, "John is going to
go through the folder and show
you his work." Let the work speak
for itself.

6. Ask the parent if he/she has questions.

7. Identify the follow-up strategies
and tools to be used.

8. Thank the parent for coming.

Questions/Techniques to Facilitate the Conference

1. Stay away from "why" questions.
Instead, begin with these words:
when, how, what, which. For
example: "When he did that, what
did he want? How will that help
him be more successful? How will

that help him win? What have you noticed? How would you like to do the follow-up? Which way would work best for you? What is the worst-case scenario? What is the best-case scenario? How would you like to have this resolved? What plan could we use?"

2. STAY AWAY FROM STATEMENTS. Use data and questions.

3. Identify the fuzzy nouns and pronouns (*everyone, they, them, all the parents, all the students, women, men, kids, etc.*). If those words are in the conversation, ask this question: "Specifically who or which …?"

4. Identify vague qualifiers. Example: "It's better." ("Better than what?")

5. Identify fuzzy adverbs. Example: "He always has a bad teacher." ("Always? Has there ever been a time when the teacher was good?")

6. Identify the emotion in a statement. For example: "You're racist!" ("I sense that you feel the school is unfair and insensitive. Can you give me a specific example that would help me understand?")

7. Identify the hidden rules or beliefs (*should, must, can't, have to, ought to, should not, mandatory*). Example: "What would happen if you did? What stops you?"

8. Identify the parameters of the school. Example: "We do that to keep children safe." Or: "Just as we don't allow other parents to come in and tell us what to do with your child, we cannot allow you to dictate procedure for other people's children."

Phrases to Use with Parents

IN POVERTY	IN AFFLUENCE
This will help him/her win more often.	This coping strategy will help him/her be more successful in the corporate world.
This will keep him/her from being cheated.	Responsibility and decision making are learned behaviors. We can give him/her the competitive edge as an adult by learning these behaviors now.
This will help him/her be respected and in control.	This will keep him/her safe.
This will help him/her be tougher and stronger.	This will help him/her have the advantage.
His/her mind is a tool and a weapon that no one can take away.	This is a legal requirement.
This will help him/her be smarter.	This is an investment in your child's future success.
This will help keep you safe when you are old.	He/she will need processes/skills/content in the work world.
This is a legal requirement.	
I know that you love and care about your child very much or you would not have come to see me.	

CONCLUSION

The concepts that schools have used for so long to involve parents tend to be one-way, linear, and meeting-oriented. Just as advertisers have discovered that multiple messages and mediums are required to influence buyers, we must also use the scaffolding of relationships, interventions, activities, mutual respect, conflict resolution, and targeted assistance to create communities of support.

BIBLIOGRAPHY

Rosario, Jose R. (2003). *Final Narrative Report: September 1, 2002-August 31, 2003.* Hispanic Education Center, El Puente Project. Indianapolis, IN. Funded by Lumina Foundation for Education.

Wehlage, G.G., Rutter, R.A., Smith, G.A., Lesko, N., & Fernandez, R.R. (1989). *Reducing the Risk: Schools as Communities of Support.* Philadelphia, PA: Falmer Press.

Ruby K. Payne, Ph.D., founder and president of **aha!** Process, Inc. (1994), with more than 30 years experience as a professional educator, has been sharing her insights about the impact of poverty —and how to help educators and other professionals work effectively with individuals from poverty—in more than a thousand workshop settings through North America, Canada, and Australia.

Her seminal work, *A Framework for Understanding Poverty,* teaches the hidden rules of economic class and spreads the message that, despite the obstacles poverty can create in all types of interaction, there are specific strategies for overcoming them. Since publishing *Framework* in 1995, Dr. Payne also has written or co-authored nearly a dozen books surrounding these issues in such areas as education, social services, the workplace, faith communities, and leadership.

More information on her book, *A Framework for Understanding Poverty,* can be found on her website, www.ahaprocess.com.

PARENT/TEACHER CONFERENCE FORM WITH STUDENT

Student name_____ Date_____ Time_____

Parent name_____ Teacher_____

PURPOSE OF THE CONFERENCE (CHECK AS MANY AS APPLY)

_____ scheduled teacher/parent conference

_____ student achievement issue

_____ parent-initiated

_____ discipline issue

_____ social/emotional issue

WHAT IS THE DESIRED GOAL OF THE CONFERENCE?

WHAT DATA WILL I OR THE STUDENT SHOW THE PARENT? Student work, discipline referrals, student planning documents?

WHAT QUESTIONS NEED TO BE ASKED? WHAT ISSUES NEED TO BE DISCUSSED?

WHAT FOLLOW-UP TOOLS AND STRATEGIES WILL BE IDENTIFIED?

BIBLIOGRAPHY

Bibliography

Berliner, D.C. (1988). *Implications of Studies of Expertise in Pedagogy for Teacher Education and Evaluation*. Paper presented 1988 Educational Testing Service Invitational Conference on New Directions for Teacher Assessment. New York, NY.

Berne, Eric. (1996). *Games People Play: The Basic Handbook of Transactional Analysis*. New York, NY: Ballantine Books.

Bloom, Benjamin. (1976). *Human Characteristics and School Learning*. New York, NY: McGraw-Hill Book Company.

Caine, Renate Nummela, & Caine, Goeffrey. (1991). *Making Connections: Teaching and the Human Brain*. Alexandria, VA: ASCD.

Collins, Bryn C. (1997). *Emotional Unavailability: Recognizing It, Understanding It, and Avoiding Its Trap*. Lincolnwood, IL: NTC/Contemporary Publishing Company.

Covey, Stephen R. (1989). *The Seven Habits of Highly Effective People:Powerful Lessons in Personal Change*. New York, NY: Simon and Schuster.

Feuerstein, Reuven, et al. (1980). *Instrumental Enrichment: An Intervention Program for Cognitive Modifiability*. Glenview, IL: Scott, Foresman & Co.

Idol, Lorna, & Jones, B.F., eds. (1991). *Educational Values and Cognitive Instruction: Implications for Reform*. Hillsdale, NJ: Lawrence Erlbaum Associates.

Jones, B.F., Pierce, J., & Hunter, B. (1988). *Teaching Students to Construct Graphic Representations. Educational Leadership*. Volume 46 (4), 20-25.

Marzano, Robert J. & Arrendondo, Daisy. (1986). *Tactics for Thinking*. Aurora, CO: MCREL.

Palinscar, A.S., & Brown, A.L. (1984). *The Reciprocal Teaching of Comprehension-Fostering and Comprehension-Monitoring Activities. Cognition and Instruction*. Volume 1 (2). 117-175.

Sharron, Howard, & Coulter, Martha. (1994). *Changing Children's Minds: Feuerstein's Revolution in the Teaching of Intelligence*. Exeter, Great Britain: BPC Wheatons Ltd.

Wolin, Steven J., & Wolin, Sybil. (1994). *The Resilient Self: How Survivors of Troubled Families Rise Above Adversity*. New York, NY: Villard Books.

Eye-openers at ...

Interested in more information?

We invite you to our website, www.ahaprocess.com to join our **aha!** News List!

Receive the latest income and poverty statistics free when you join! Then receive **aha!** News, and periodic updates!

Also on the website:

- Success stories from our participants—from schools, social services, and businesses
- Three new workshops!
- Four Trainer Certification programs
- An up-to-date listing of our books & videos
- A convenient online store
- Dr. Ruby Payne's U.S. National Tour dates
- A videoclip of Dr. Payne
- News articles from around the country

And more at …

www.ahaprocess.com

www.ahaprocess.com
PO Box 727, Highlands, TX 77562-0727
(800) 424-9484; fax: (281) 426-8705
store@ahaprocess.com

ORDER FORM

UPS SHIP TO ADDRESS: (no post office boxes, please)

NAME: _____ E-mail _____

ORGANIZATION: _____

ADDRESS: _____

CITY/STATE/ZIP: _____

TELEPHONE: _____ FAX: _____

QTY	TITLE	1-4 Copies	5+ Copies*	Total
	A Framework for Understanding Poverty	22.00	15.00	
	A Framework for Understanding Poverty Workbook	7.00	7.00	
	Understanding Learning *(for Day 2 training order set below)*	7.00	7.00	
	Learning Structures Workbook *(for Day 2 training, order set below)*	7.00	7.00	
	Understanding Learning/Learning Structures workbook (bundled set for Day 2)	10.00	10.00	
	A Framework for Understanding Poverty Audio Workshop Kit (includes Day 1 & 2 8 CDs –and 4 books listed above) **S/H: $10.50**	225.00	225.00	
	Un Marco Para Entender La Pobreza	22.00	15.00	
	A Framework for Understanding Poverty Audio CD Set/Book	35.00	35.00	
	Putting the Pieces Together workbook (replaces Application of Learning Structures)	10.00	10.00	
	A Picture Is Worth a Thousand Words	18.00	15.00	
	Berrytales – Plays in One Act	25.00	20.00	
	Bridges Out of Poverty: Strategies for Professionals & Communities	22.00	15.00	
	Changing Children's Minds	30.00	30.00	
	Crossing the Tracks for Love	14.95	14.95	
	Daily Math Practice for Virginia SOLs – Grade 4	22.00	15.00	
	Daily Math Skills Review Grade 4- practice for mastery of math standards	22.00	15.00	
	Getting Ahead in a Just Gettin'-By World & Facilitator Notes (set)	25.00	25.00	
	Getting Ahead in a Just Gettin'-By World *(after purchasing a set)*	15.00	15.00	
	Getting Ahead in a Just Gettin'-By World Facilitator Notes (after set)	10.00	10.00	
	Hear Our Cry: Boys in Crisis	22.00	15.00	
	Hidden Rules of Class at Work	22.00	15.00	
	Living on a Tightrope: a Survival Handbook for Principals	22.00	15.00	
	Mr. Base Ten Invents Mathematics	22.00	15.00	
	Parenting Someone Else's Child: The Foster Parents' How-To Manual	22.00	15.00	
	Removing the Mask: Giftedness in Poverty	25.00	20.00	
	Environmental Opportunity Profile (25/set-incl 1 FAQ)	25.00	25.00	
	Addit'l FAQs Environmental Opportunities Profile manual	3.00	3.00	
	Slocumb-Payne Teacher Perception Inventory (25/set)	25.00	25.00	
	Think Rather of Zebra	18.00	15.00	
	Trainer's Companion: Stories to Stimulate Reflection, Conversation, Action	22.00	15.00	
	What Every Church Member Should Know About Poverty	22.00	15.00	
	Tucker Signing Strategies Video & Manual **S/H: $8.50**	195.00	195.00	
	Tucker Signs Reference Cards on CD	25.00	25.00	
	Take-Home Books for Tucker Signing Strategies for Reading	22.00	15.00	
	Preventing School Violence – 5 videos & manual **S/H: $15.00**	995.00	995.00	
	Preventing School Violence CD – PowerPoint presentation	25.00	25.00	
	Preventing School Violence Training Manual	15.00	15.00	
	Audiotapes, What Every Church Member Should Know About Poverty	25.00	25.00	
	Meeting Standards & Raising Test Scores When You Don't Have Much Time or Money (4 videos/training manual **S/H: $15.00**	995.00	995.00	
	Meeting Standards & Raising Test Scores Training Manual	18.00	18.00	
	Meeting Standards & Raising Test Scores Resource Manual	18.00	18.00	
	Meeting Standards & Raising Test Scores CD – PowerPoint presentation	50.00	50.00	
	Rita's Stories (2 videos) **S/H: $8.50** Rita's Stories DVD **S/H: $4.50**	150.00	150.00	
	Ruby Payne Video or DVD Sampler **S/H: $4.50**	10.00	10.00	
	aha! 12 oz. mugs (white with red logo and website)	8.00	2@15.00	
	Rubygems! 16-month Planner – Educator/Parent Relationships	10.00	10+ 8.00	
	Walk-through Rubric Notepads – *Circle one:* General; Mutual Respect; Instruction; Discipline & Classroom Management, Audit for Differentiated Instruction, Assorted	5@5.00	50@30.00	

For Certified Trainers Only – Please note date/city of training:

QTY	TITLE	1-4 Copies	5+ Copies*	Total
	A Framework for Understanding Poverty Video Sets (12 modules) (Day 1 & Day 2 of Framework seminar) Circle one: VHS or DVD **S/H: $25.00**	1995.00	1995.00	
	A Framework for Understanding Poverty CD – PowerPoint presentation	50.00	50.00	
	A Framework for Understanding Poverty CD – Enhanced PowerPoint pres.	100.00	100.00	
	Bridges Out of Poverty CD – PowerPoint presentation	50.00	50.00	

Total Quantity		Subtotal	
TERMS: S/H: 1-4 books – $4.50 plus $2.00 each additional book up to 4 books, [1 calendar $2]		S/H	
5+ books – 8% of total, *(special S/H for videos). E-mail for international rates.*		Tax	
TAX: 6.25% Texas residents only Prices subject to change. Visit website for current offerings.		**Total**	

AmEx   MC   Visa   Discover

CREDIT CARD # _____ EXP. DATE _____ Signature _____

AUTHORIZATION # _____ PO # _____ (please fax PO with order) Check # _____.

*Orders placed by participants while attending U.S. National Tour or Trainer Certification are given quantity (5 or more) pricing.